Dangerous Seas

Memoirs of a Sailor Aboard a Destroyer During World War II

by

David L. Williams

Woodstock Books

Dangerous Seas

All Rights Reserved
Copyright ©1998 by David L. Williams

No part of this book may be used or reproduced or transmitted in any form or by any means, electronic or mechanical, including photocopying, recording, or by any information storage or retrieval system, except in the case of reviews, without permission in writing from the publisher. For information write to Woodstock Books, 120 West Main Street, Box 70, Plainville CT 06062.

Library of Congress Catalog Card Number 97-62358

ISBN 0-9640096-2-5

Manufactured in the United States of America
First Printing 1998

Published by
WOODSTOCK BOOKS, LLC
Plainville, CT

Dedication

To my father, Stanley T. Williams

Foreword

The momentous events of World War II, which occurred a half a century ago, are now only faint memories and footnotes to history. For my generation, however, this was a world and a time changed forever.

Now that I am much older, I feel compelled to narrate my wartime experiences. I have no illusions about the world's interest in these memoirs, yet I cherish the hope that my children and their children will some day read this tale of youth and perhaps benefit by it.

Finally, history is a witness to the passing of time. It illuminates the past and often provides guidance for the future. Perhaps this story will contribute to some distant good, the fruition of which one may never live to see.

Acknowledgement

This story would not have been possible were it not for the assistance and encouragement of an old friend, Professor Alexander G. Medlicott, Jr., of Piermont, New Hampshire.

D.L.W

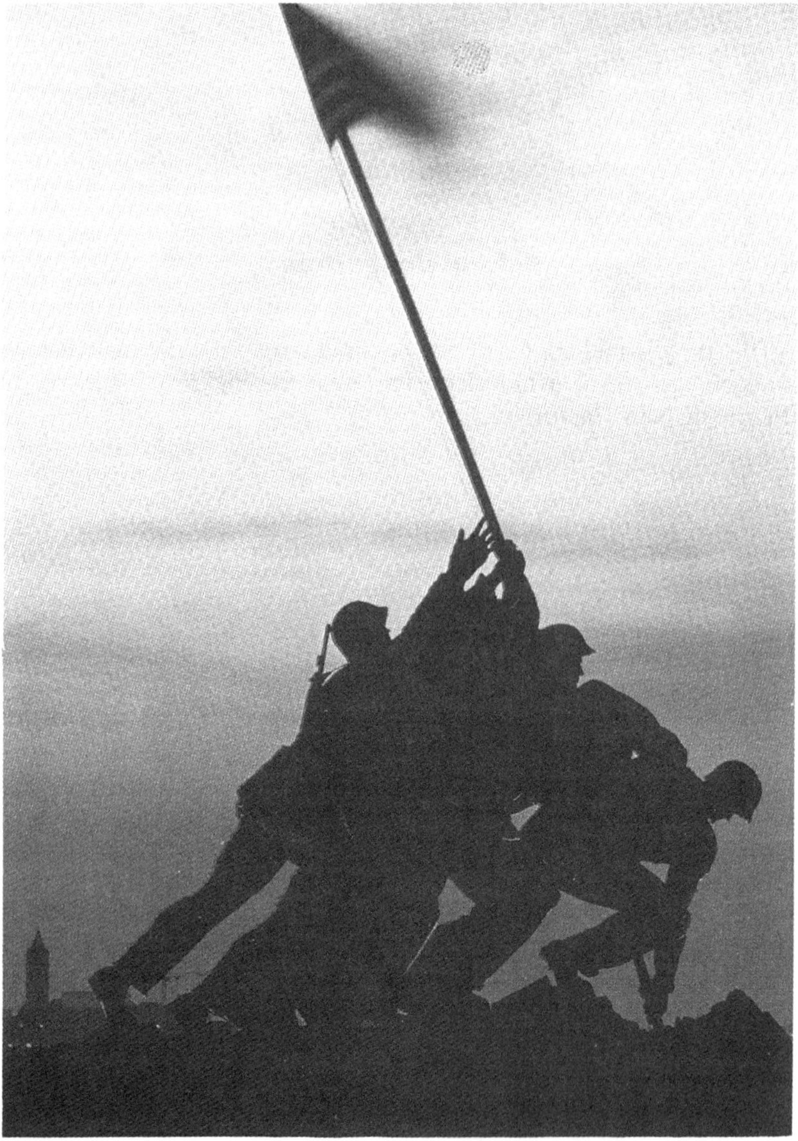

Introduction

In August of 1945, Japan surrendered unconditionally. World War II was officially over. Within a month the navy announced plans to demobilize and speedily return to civilian life some 3,000,000 men and women. In March, 1946, like so many other veterans, I was discharged from the navy after serving more than three years.

On that day I left Lido Beach, Long Island, a discharge center, and took the train to my home in Hamden, Connecticut. Still in uniform, I was proudly wearing a gold honorable discharge button, which servicemen affectionately called the "ruptured duck." In addition, I brought with me my only worldly possessions: a full sea bag and a captured Japanese rifle. As the train pulled into the railroad station, I caught my first glimpse through the window of my father anxiously waiting for me. I bounded off the train and we greeted one another in a warm embrace. After so many months away it was a wonderful feeling to be home again. My military career was over. At age 24 I was eager to pursue life once more.

During those early post-war days, both the Federal Government and the State of Connecticut offered benefits for returning veterans. Connecticut provided a bonus of $300; the Federal Government established an income program for unemployed servicemen. Consequently, and with some guilt, I accepted the $300 from the state and joined the "52 – 20 Club," as it was popularly called. I received $20.00 per week, a princely sum in those days, up to a maximum of 52 weeks, while seeking a job.

During this adjustment to civilian life, my father, a professor of English at Yale, and I had many talks about the war. He served in the American Expeditionary Force, (AEF) as a second lieutenant in France during World War I. Upon his return home in 1918, he also brought souvenirs: a German helmet and a Luger pistol. As a young boy in the 1920s, I remember wearing the German helmet during neighborhood "war games." My older brother and I knew about the Luger pistol, which my father had wisely hidden. One day we decided to find the Luger in our attic. But we were unsuccessful. Years later my mother confessed that she removed it from its hiding place and secretly threw it into the Quinnipiac River.

During one of our discussions, I gave my father my wartime diary to read. After reviewing it, he recommended that I document these events in narrative form.

At the time I was pursuing two possible options for my future. I had applied for admission, and was accepted at an art school in New York City. I also had a year and a half left to complete my liberal arts education at Wesleyan University in Middletown, Connecticut. I chose to return to

Wesleyan. My father's recommendation about my memoirs was not taken up at that time.

Now, fifty years later and in my retirement, my diary somehow reappeared. As I poke into these events of five decades ago, I find the ashes of recollection have again been stirred. Thus, I have decided to complete this project. These memoirs are affectionately dedicated to my wife, Fran; my children Linda and Susan; their children, Sarah, Kathleen, and Chelsea; my former shipmates; and to the memory of my father, who originally suggested this task so many years ago.

Dangerous Seas

Wesleyan University and the V-12 Program

In the fall of 1941 I had just turned nineteen when I began my freshman year at Wesleyan University. That September I joined the Class of 1945, along with 136 classmates. In those days tradition required all freshman to wear a red and black knit tie and a red and black freshman beanie. This attire was expected to be worn for the fall semester, unless Wesleyan was lucky enough to beat Amherst and Williams in the "Little Three" football rivalry. These were exciting and carefree days crowded with football games, house parties, fraternity rushing, fraternity living, various campus activities, and occasional weekend trips to Smith College, Mount Holyoke, and Connecticut College.

In contrast, however, 1941 was a year filled with explosive events. World War II had begun in Europe. Hitler's victorious armies had defeated France in a matter of weeks and began dominating all Western Europe. Millions were enslaved by Nazi Germany. England stood alone in her darkest hour. It was a time in history when the human spirit was unmercifully ground under the iron heel of barbarism and terror. It was Winston Churchill, standing alone, who courageously resisted the tyrant's might. He mobilized the English language and sent it into battle. The splendor of his words appeared to ignite a flame of inspiration in freedom's gravest hour.

On February 9, 1941, in a radio address to the American people, Churchill asked the United States for financial aid with these prophetic words: "Give us your faith and your blessing, and, under Providence, all will be well. We shall not fail or falter; we shall not weaken or tire. Neither the sudden shock of battle, nor the long-drawn trials of vigilance and exertion will wear us down. Give us the tools and we will finish the job."

In Asia, Japan's military had conquered Manchuria and the eastern coast of China. Moreover, the Japanese Navy became a growing threat to her Pacific neighbors, including the United States. At home, President Roosevelt froze Japan's assets and evacuated 2,000 Japanese-Americans from our west coast. He also signed the Lend-Lease Act authorizing the sending of war materials to our friends abroad.

But Americans at home were occupied with other matters. Joe Louis, known as the "Brown Bomber," was heavyweight champion of the world, and Joe DiMaggio, of the New York Yankees, set a baseball record by hitting safely in 56 consecutive games. Ted Williams, of the Boston Red Sox, had a .401 batting average in 1941. Today, both records are still standing.

This was also the swing band era. Couples throughout the country flocked to ballrooms to listen and dance to jazz. Colleges and universities selected name bands for their spring proms: men in tails and women in formal gowns danced to the music of Glenn Miller, the Dorsey Brothers, Artie Shaw, Count Basie, Duke Ellington, Stan Kenton, and Woody Herman. Favorite dance tunes were "In The Mood," "Tuxedo Junction," "Marie," "Lady Be Good," "Muskrat Ramble," "Sing, Sing, Sing," " Blue Skies," and ''Stardust.''

On Sunday, December 7, 1941, my college roommate, Bob Newell, and I were invited to lunch with Wesleyan's president, James McConaughy. I was asked to attend only because Bob's father was an influential trustee of the University. During the formal lunch, one of the Japanese servants, who was waiting on us nervously, interrupted our meal by repeating one of the most startling radio reports. Japan had just bombed Pearl Harbor. We were suddenly at war, but no one at the dining room table knew where Pearl Harbor was. The next day Roosevelt appeared before a joint session of Congress to ask for a declaration of war against Japan. And on December 11th, United States declared war on Germany and Italy.

Almost overnight this series of events would forever change our lives. Immediately all reserves were called to service. The nation's draft system was expanded to provide a pool of draftees for the army, and industrial plants throughout the country began the manufacture of armaments. Military camps were enlarged and new ones were hurriedly constructed to handle the flood of draftees.

On the civilian front, each coastal town and village enlisted air raid wardens demanding after-dark black-outs; automobiles had their headlights partially covered with tape and black paint. There were rumors about the Japanese bombing and invading the west coast. On the east coast, lighted cities were blacked out to eliminate silhouettes that might be useful to German submarines. In time, enemy submarines would torpedo ships forming convoys only a few miles off the Cape Cod Canal. Hundreds of private yachts were requisitioned by the government and turned over to the Coast Guard for off-shore patrol during the war's duration.

Military convoys soon crowded our highways. The nation's railroads transported military supplies to both coasts. Troop trains became commonplace. Almost every eligible male was in uniform. Overnight our country became an armed camp.

On the civilian front, shortages quickly appeared. Army tanks replaced new cars. There was a shortage of rubber, butter, meat, fish, silk stockings, cigarettes, coffee, and gasoline. Local ration boards were established to control civilian needs. Motorists with "A" coupons were restricted to three gallons of gasoline weekly. Doctors, defense workers, and others who could justify a vital need for transportation were issued "C" or "D" cards which

Dangerous Seas

provided additional gasoline.

If one knew where to go, gas coupons were available on the black market. At Wesleyan, the custodian of our fraternity house, Bill Zarro, somehow produced extra gas coupons for several fraternity brothers, so our week-end trips to women's colleges continued.

Patriotism swept the country. At Wesleyan, like many other campuses, students gave up their studies and volunteered to serve. Recruiting offices throughout the country were swamped with enlistments. Other young men joined newly-formed officer's candidate schools and stayed in class until they were called up.

Wesleyan became a training ground for the Naval Air Corps and the Naval Reserve. I immediately applied for the Naval Reserve, designated V-12, and awaited induction, which came the summer of 1943. Exclusive of certain navy requirements, I continued my college courses at Wesleyan in a sailor suit with the lowest rank in the navy—apprentice seaman.

The refined college life, which I had taken for granted, was quickly changing. I moved from the spacious and relaxed quarters of our fraternity house to a small, spartan four-bunk room on the third floor of North College, a campus dormitory. To make my new home more nautical, the navy changed the name of our dormitory to *USS North College*. Our new routine required mustering at 6:00 a.m. each morning, marching about the campus, enduring extensive calisthenics, and bed checks at night. Slowly I was losing my freedom.

Further changes occurred in my selection of courses. I had to give up several humanity studies in exchange for required courses in mathematics and physics. Our physics class was run by a Professor Eaton. The students referred to him affectionately as the "Moth" or "Moth Eaton." "The Moth" was a solemn, humorless man who delighted in making the subject difficult. In his first lecture before a large class he said, "In the broadest sense physics is concerned with all aspects of nature on both the macroscopic and submicroscopic levels." He continued, "Its scope of study encompasses not only the behavior of objects under the action of given forces but also the nature and origin of gravitational, electromagnetic and nuclear force fields." For a liberal arts student who wasn't always attentive in class, this introduction was the beginning of bad news.

One student who sat next to me in physics class was Chuck Ash, a fraternity brother. Chuck was a popular, laid-back athlete who was on the track and swimming teams. When it came to the sciences, even though he studied, he simply couldn't understand physics.

One of our first experiments in the physics lab involved a block of wood about six inches square suspended by string from the ceiling. The "Moth" stood back and fired a .22 caliber bullet into the block. The impact of the bullet instantly spun the block outward from its original position. By calculating the speed of the bullet and applying certain formulas, the student was supposed to measure the bullet's impact. In desperation I looked at Chuck and saw his glazed look. We were both totally lost. When the course ended, I somehow managed to get a "D." Chuck Ash received an "F." He was required to repeat the course and received once again, an "F." To this day I can still remember the first formula we had to memorize. It was F = MxA (force equals mass times acceleration). I quickly learned that I would never become a successful nuclear scientist.

It soon became clear, however, that the combination of required math courses (plus physics), my inability to study seriously, and my immaturity at the time, all adversely affected my scholastic record. At the end of the fall semester the administration wisely decided that I lacked the qualities required to become an officer and a gentlemen. Consequently, in the winter of 1943, I received a pink slip ordering me to proceed at once to Sampson Naval Base in upper New York State in the winter of 1943. I was to continue my military career as an enlisted man, a life which would prove to be vastly different from that of a commissioned officer. What followed would change me from a pink-checked, naive youth to a fully-grown man of some maturity.

Boot Camp

The transition from a sheltered, genteel college life and the V-12 Naval Reserve to basic training as an enlisted man in the real United States Navy was not only a rude awakening, but a stunning culture shock. In the winter of 1943, I boarded my first troop train in New York's Grand Central Station. Our destination was Sampson Naval Base in Sampson, New York. Each passenger car was clogged with enlisted men who had been on liberty in the city. For many it was their last fling before going on active duty. Some would be assigned to the fleet; others would proceed to a petty officers' school for further training.

I was relegated to an old passenger car which had seen far better days. It was shabby, dirty, and poorly heated. Once underway, the windows rattled and frigid air rushed in from every crack and corner. We sat upright on hard cane seats. The narrow isle was cluttered with sea bags, luggage, rubbish, discarded food, empty liquor bottles, and beer cans. During our journey into the night the monotonous clatter of the train was often interrupted by the sounds of someone singing to the accompaniment of a guitar. Further down the isle several crap games started among boisterous drunks who settled arguments with their fists. Suddenly I heard the sound of a shattered window. The shore patrol quickly arrived, restored law and order and removed the assailants. For the rest of the journey there was no heat and sleep was impossible.

At dawn our troop train slowly rattled to a stop. We had reached our destination—Sampson Naval Base, my home for the next six weeks. At the railway station a navy band greeted us with "Anchors Aweigh" as I stumbled off the train, tired, dirty, and red-eyed. To the assertive orders of a boatswain's mate, I mustered in the cold morning air, and our unit marched to a mess hall for our first breakfast.

The first order of the day was the distribution of GI clothing for all recruits. In line we moved slowly past storekeepers who issued one set of dress blues and one set of undressed blues with bell-bottom trousers. In accordance with navy customs, bell-bottom trousers were adorned with thirteen buttons across the front. We were told that the buttons represented the original thirteen colonies. (Navy tradition was one thing, but getting your pants on and off in a hurry was another). In addition, we were issued a set of white uniforms, three white caps, one dark woolen navy cap with "U.S. Navy" on the band, two sets of blue dungarees for work details, one black kerchief, a pair of puttees for guard duty and parades, socks, underwear (known as "skivvies"), two pairs of black thick-sole shoes, black gloves, and a heavy wool double-breasted pea jacket.

At boot camp I had the lowest grade in the navy, apprentice seaman. And at the completion of boot camp, one's rating automatically advanced to seaman second class. With good behavior and a few acquired skills, seaman first class eventually could be achieved.

A seaman with a white stripe around the right shoulder identified him as a deck hand. A red stripe signified a fireman who worked below deck. Firemen were frequently referred to by deck hands as "snipes." Petty officers, such as yeomen, signalmen, quartermasters, boatswains, and the like could advance as high as chief petty officer. Infrequently, an enlisted man was promoted to a commissioned officer in rank. In navy lingo he was called a "mustang."

The highest rating for enlisted men in the navy was chief petty officer. Aboard ship, chiefs had their own living quarters, remained by themselves, and, in the eyes of many enlisted men, had earned the "softest" job in the navy. Because most of them were regular navy and not reservists, they were treated differentially by commissioned and non-commissioned reservists. Because chiefs could delegate all manual labor to lower ratings, some enlisted men considered chief petty officers as professional "gold bricks."

My temporary home at Sampson was a two-story wooden barracks characterized by dreary uniformity and plainness. I lived on the first floor in a large room filled with triple decker bunks. At one end of the building was a small yeoman's office outfitted with several dilapidated chairs and a small wooden desk used for guard duty and administrative details. The heating system in the barracks consisted of three potbellied, coal-burning stoves. Men standing watch were responsible for keeping a lighted fire in the stoves at all times. Nearby, our bathroom (or head) was an endless row of sinks, showers, and toilets. With more than a hundred men using these crowded facilities, I soon learned there was no privacy in the United States Navy.

When we weren't involved in military drill or forced marches of endurance, we were subjected to endless lectures and basic training films covering a variety of subjects. We learned navy lingo, etiquette, and basic seamanship. We could identify by silhouette enemy ships and planes. We had courses on first aid. We put out oil fires and entered a gas chamber filled with gas. Once inside the instructors made us remove our gas masks so we could react to tear gas. I immediately bolted out of the chamber coughing and gagging. My eyes watered and I couldn't see anything for a few moments. The chief boatswain in charge took great pleasure watching his boots suffer.

As recruits we were subjected to graphic training films covering crabs, lice, gonorrhea, syphilis, clap, and herpes, coupled with descriptive pictures of all these social diseases. Old navy traditions were hammered into the minds of all boots. Walls became "bulkheads," floors were "decks," stairs were "ladders," latrines were "heads." A rumor was "scuttlebutt." "Joe" was coffee and "Old Joe" was a sexually transmitted disease. Cleaning up

Dangerous Seas

the barracks was a "field day.' You said "Aye, aye, sir," instead of "Yes, sir." On a ship we could identify the main deck, poop deck, and the forecastle (pronounced "folksell.") We learned that battleships were named after states, aircraft carriers after famous Americans (Benjamin Franklin) or a well-known historical event (Coral Sea, Midway, and Yorktown), cruisers after cities, and destroyers usually after naval heroes.

Navy protocol required all officers and enlisted men to salute the captain of the ship on every occasion, and enlisted men saluted all officers junior to the captain on their first daily meeting. In addition, all salutes in passing were initiated by enlisted men. And when boarding or leaving a ship, we were taught to salute the colors on the fantail and again the officer of the deck at the gangway. I quickly learned, however, that most of these formalities were abandoned at sea.

In 1943 the official basic monthly pay for enlisted men was:

Chief Petty Officer	$138.00
Petty Officer First Class	$114.00
Petty Officer Second Class	$ 96.00
Petty Officer Third Class	$ 78.00
Seaman First Class	$ 66.00
Seaman Second Class	$ 54.00
Apprentice Seaman	$ 50.00

As a seaman with all expenses paid, I was able to set aside monthly savings during the course of my naval career because I was at sea most of the time. When ashore, I found USOs in various cities provided excellent entertainment, good food, and at times attractive, patriotic women. Finally, the ports of call in the Pacific Theatre (apart from Hawaii) were for the most part desolate and inhabited by only primitive natives.

The classification of officers below the captain of a typical warship was as follows:

Executive Officer
First Lieutenant and Damage Control Officer
Navigator
Gunnery Officer
Engineering Officer
Officer of The Deck
Medical Officer
Supply Officer

Standing watch at sea required a thorough understanding how the navy ran its day. All boots had to familiarize themselves with each watch and the way the navy kept time as shown below:

Mid-watch	midnight to 4:00 a.m.
Morning watch	4:00 a.m. to 8:00 a.m.
Forenoon watch	8:00 a.m. to 12:00 p.m.

    Afternoon watch   *noon to 4:00 p.m.*
    Dog watch   *4:00 a.m. to 8:00 a.m.*
    First watch   *8:00 p.m. to midnight*

    Sampson Naval Base was the loneliest, most barren, God-forsaken spot in the world. I arrived there in the middle of winter when bitter, cold winds continuously swept across our camp grounds making outdoor activities a miserable experience. But we continued to muster in mud and snow for our marches of endurance and daily drills. Our base was divided into units; my Unit was D and housed slightly more than 15,000 boots. Moreover, Unit D was filled with college men, who like myself had washed out of V-12. They arrived mostly from New England colleges and universities. With this common background, I had short-term friendships with men from St. Lawrence, Bowdoin, Williams, and Amherst. In time, however, most of these men departed for petty officer schools. This same group of ex-college men were in top physical shape because of prior V-12 training programs. As a result, all men in Unit D excelled in basketball, wrestling, and boxing.

    Boxing as a sport was always of interest to me. As a boy, I followed professional boxing and kept a scrap book of famous fighters. In those days I watched with eagerness the careers of champions such as Jack Sharkey, Primo Canera, Max Baer, Max Schmeling, Billy Conn, and Joe Louis. Recognizing this interest, my father hired a Yale graduate student named Ted Zunder to give my brother and me boxing lessons every Sunday afternoon. We were impressed with Ted's credentials, since he claimed to have been a sparring partner of Gene Tunney, former heavyweight champion of the world.

    With this background I decided to try out for the boxing team of Unit D. At the time I weighed only 145 pounds, stood 6' 2", was in good condition, and had a long reach. (I wear a thirty-six inch sleeve.) While these were not imposing fighter qualifications, I did manage to achieve some early successes largely due to the inexperience of my opponents. One afternoon, however, I was pitted against a rough-looking, muscular, barrel-chested character who stood a tad over five feet. (I subsequently learned that my opponent in civilian life was a longshoreman who loaded and unloaded ships in Brooklyn, New York.) When the bell rang, my adversary rushed from his corner and immediately broke through my defenses and pummeled my body unmercifully. At the end of our three-round bout I was still standing, but I was badly bruised and thoroughly beaten. After that memorable episode, my boxing career came to an abrupt end. I decided to hang up my boxing gloves permanently.

    As a boot, I will always remember my first medical exam at Sampson. While in formation one morning our chief announced that those individuals whose last name began with W were to fall out and march to the medical

Dangerous Seas

building for a complete physical. Once there, a pharmacist mate told us to strip and stand in line where we were herded nude, like cattle, through a series of rooms for processing. I felt like a piece of meat being processed for slaughter in a stockyard. We received shots in both arms, underwent a cursory eye examination, had blood tests, blood pressure readings, and voided into specimen bottles. Still nude, we were lined up in a long row at which point a doctor, accompanied by a chief pharmacist, passed by asking each boot to cough as he checked for hernias. We were then ordered to bend over and spread our cheeks so that the same doctor could check for hemorrhoids. As he came down the line inspecting each patient with a flashlight, he paused behind the boot next to me and said in a low voice, "My God, sailor, are you trying to hoard toilet paper?"

All recruits were required to have a dental examination. Again, by alphabet we stood in long lines to be examined by three navy dentists. Because there were too few dentists and an unending supply of recruits, there wasn't time to treat dental problems selectively. Many boots had never received proper dental care. Others had never seen a dentist. Extractions were commonplace. When my turn in the dental chair came, I was given a rudimentary exam and the dentist quickly said, "You have an impacted wisdom tooth which should be extracted. While we are at it, I'll remove the other three as well." He quickly filled out a slip setting a future date for the extractions, handed it to me, and without pause called for his next victim. I never returned for this appointment. Some fifty years later, I still have three of my four wisdom teeth.

Perhaps one of the most humbling experiences to one's ego is the first boot haircut. One morning at muster, our boatswain announced that ship's company was in need of a GI haircut, so we were herded to a barber shop for our first shearing. Four barbers, surrounded by piles of hair, were busy skinning the recruits one by one. When my turn came to climb into the chair, I immediately felt the rapid and firm strokes of clippers passing over my scalp. In less than a minute I became a skinned rabbit to the taunting chorus of onlookers who shouted, "You'll be sorry," "Hey, skinhead," and "You look much better with your ears lowered." The attending boatswain added his two cents by saying, "You were born bald and under my care you will remain bald." When it was over, I began to realize how one's looks were altered by a shiny scalp. I slunk out of the barber shop humiliated. I had lost all my dignity.

The navy's philosophy at Sampson was simple: a busy boot is a happy boot. I quickly learned that it was a tactical blunder to finish an assignment too soon. It was a discredit to the ethics of goldbricking. If a superior saw a recruit idle or relaxing in any way, that became an invitation for work. One cold, winter afternoon, I was caught at ease in our head by roving boatswains who immediately put me on assignment. That afternoon I was given my next task. Ten boots, myself included, were ordered to the mess hall where under close supervision we formed a butt squad. We were told to circle the mess hall and pick up all discarded butts and place them carefully in paper bags. Unit D's mess hall serviced well over 3,000 men. In those days everyone smoked.

When the task was completed to the satisfaction of our superiors, I returned to my barrack to find that I was assigned to KP duty for the next three days. My new job was highly specialized. I cleaned and scrubbed garbage cans after every meal with soap, hot water, and steel brushes.

My days as a boot at Sampson were now drawing to a close. I would soon be promoted to Seaman Second Class giving me an extra stripe on my sleeves and a raise in pay to $54.00 per month. No longer would I be a recruit.

On the day of departure from Sampson, we had a final field day in our barrack. And later that morning a dress parade with a military band was held. The reviewing stand was filled with dignitaries, including the commandant of the base. The ceremony came to a conclusion with our unit standing at attention on a cold winter morning, at which time a well-fed navy captain appeared at the lectern. He gave a long-winded speech to his captive audience, talking endlessly about "upholding navy tradition," and "wearing our uniforms proudly." Standing there in the icy weather, my mind wandered off. I thought about my college classes where a professor's lecture usually ended with the ringing of a bell. Suddenly a navy band began to play. The speaker had finished, and I returned to reality.

Our unit then marched to the railroad depot and boarded another troop train headed south. As the locomotive slowly pulled away from the station, I was happy to bid Sampson Naval Base a final farewell. And I began at once to think about my next naval assignment, sonar school in Key West, Florida

Dangerous Seas

Key West

Our troop train, crowded, hot, and dirty, rumbled slowly through New York, Pennsylvania, Maryland, Virginia, North and South Carolina, through Georgia to Florida. Our destination was Miami, a place that sailors called a "good liberty town." Along the way our train made frequent stops for food supplies; hawkers appeared along the tracks to peddle snacks to supplement our navy meals. At some of the stations, various women's organizations greeted us with coffee and doughnuts. As a Yankee boy far from home, I appreciated these generous, patriotic groups and wondered if this was what southern hospitality was all about.

After four long days our troop train finally pulled into Miami. To my surprise I was immediately assigned to a military bus that left at once for Key West. It was a great disappointment to me that I was unable to visit Miami and test a "good liberty town."

Key West is the southernmost settlement in the continental limits of the United States. An overseas highway connects the mainland to the Keys by some forty bridges which are several miles long. As I knew it, Key West was a tropical town with a unique blend of Cubans, West Indians, Bahamians, and Americans. As a seaport, it was known for its fish, crabs, lobster tails, shrimp, and sea turtles. The few times that I ventured from the base, I would always have soup and turtle steak, a rare delicacy!

The town of Key West was totally dominated by a thriving naval base, and its main street was overcrowded with sailors on liberty looking for a good time. The Chamber of Commerce may have championed the preserved homes of Ernest Hemingway and John Audubon, but its main thoroughfare was a string of dirty, jam-packed bars, sleazy women, shabby tattoo parlors, squalid restaurants, and bawdy, honky-tonk dance halls. It was a common sight to see young sailors standing in line waiting patiently to have a tattoo artist imprint on a shoulder or forearm a nautical insignia as a badge of honor. I recall one very young sailor proudly displaying his bare shoulder revealing the inked words, "For God, Mother, and Country" printed over an anchor crossed with an American flag.

During the winter of 1943, the weather in Key West was warm, balmy, and beautiful. The naval base was spacious, modern, and had excellent facilities and government-run stores. My daily activities were divided between classroom lectures on sonar and afternoon trips at sea on patrol boats and small sub chasers. In the classroom we spent hours learning the different sounds of submarines approaching and moving away from our sonar gear. We were also taught to recognize the difference between submarine noises and other underwater disturbances, such as schools of fish and whales. The training aboard small patrol boats was always pleasurable, because I was finally at sea. I stood watch, took my turn on the sonar gear

11

tracking friendly submarines, and thoroughly enjoyed my seagoing jaunts. As a boy growing up and spending summers on Cape Cod, I had a mystical fascination for the sea. Now, my daily trips into the beautiful Gulf Stream revealed once more a world resplendent in changing colors. As the waves flung their spray against the sun, the ocean's colors constantly changed from blue to blue-green to grey against a sky of dazzling blue. Temporarily at least, it was a world not harassed by man. I spent hours watching the unending and mysterious undulation of the ocean periodically being interrupted by a passing school of fish. And high above our ship I observed occasional land birds migrating on unknown journeys. Nearby I could see and hear spiraling flights of sea gulls diving and climbing effortlessly among the hurrying waves. For a time I became part of nature. But in reality I had naval responsibilities. The sonarman's job was to listen to an endless "ping"—nothing more than high-frequency sound waves emitted from the ship's hull. The direction of the undersea search was controlled by the sonarman who scanned the ocean from the ship's beams forward to the bow. This procedure was repeated endlessly whenever the ship was underway. If these impulses struck a submerged target, such as a lurking submarine, an echo with a different tone returned. By measuring the length of time between the "ping" and the returning echo, the sonarman could determine with some accuracy the actual distance and movement of the target. Concurrently, the traveling target was electrically plotted on a graph. When the ship passed over and was slightly beyond the target, an order was given to the fantail, "Drop one! Drop Two! Drop three!"

Instantly, heavy ash cans loaded with explosives were rolled off the stern. And at the same time, K-guns located on the starboard and port quarters propelled smaller missiles called "hedgehogs" into the sea. After a delay of ten to fifteen seconds, this wide pattern of depth charges exploded beneath the water with a deep, turbulent rumble. The ship shuddered from these blasts and astern the ocean boiled angrily and rose up to great heights. These detonations were capable of destroying all nearby human and animal life.

During my final days at Key West, I learned that the admiral of the base was a devout baseball fan. He was very anxious to build a winning team and sought recruits from transient enlisted personnel. Somehow word got around that during my undergraduate days I was a left-handed pitcher on Wesleyan's baseball team. I was subsequently approached by the admiral's intermediaries who suggested that I try out for the team. I was told that my reward, if chosen, would be indefinite safe duty at Key West.

This rather unusual offer started me thinking about my brief, inglorious career as a college baseball pitcher. In those days our team did little, if any, training during the spring season. We continued to smoke and drink beer and liquor at frequent house parties. Additionally, habitual bull sessions

Dangerous Seas

into the night resulted in little sleep. When my turn on the mound took place, I found that I was reasonably effective for four or five innings. Then fatigue gradually took over. I started walking batters with increasing regularity. One Saturday afternoon I was given the starting pitching assignment against the University of Connecticut. The first baseman on their team was Walt Dropo, a big, strapping farm boy from Moosup, Connecticut. He weighed close to 200 pounds and stood well over 6 feet 4 inches. He played first base, and was one of Connecticut's best all-around athletes and their team's best hitter. (Dropo eventually played first base for the Boston Red Sox and for a time hit over .400.)

As clean up hitter, Dropo batted fourth. When he came to the plate for the first time, I knew I was in trouble. From the pitcher's mound I was facing an awesome giant. I wondered how I could trick this menacing gorilla, so my first pitch was a fast ball down the middle. Instantly this giant of a man uncoiled. His bat met the ball squarely, rifling it into left center field beyond both fielders. and I immediately thought this would surely be a home run. Somehow our center fielder quickly retrieved the ball. He relayed it to the shortstop who fired it to second base. To my astonishment, Dropo, like a World War I army tank, trudged awkwardly down the first base path and rounded first base headed for second. But because of his slowness and the speed of the outfielders, he was held to a long single. Dropo's hit was the beginning of the end. His teammates began to fatten their batting averages with hits to all fields. I was benched in the third inning.

While pitching against one of our big rivals, Trinity College, I suddenly lost control and hit three batters in a row, causing Dan Jessie, the fiery Trinity coach, to rush to the home plate. He said to the umpire, "If this pitcher stays in the ball game any longer, he will cripple my entire team." I was immediately relieved and henceforth my teammates called me "Groin-ball Williams."

When it came time to try out for the Key West team, I declined the offer to display my unique left-handed pitching ability. As an excuse, I told the authorities that I wanted sea duty.

Dangerous Seas

Norfolk, Virginia

During World War II, Norfolk Naval Base was the headquarters of the United States Atlantic Fleet. Located at the mouth of Chesapeake Bay, the navy had extensive military facilities in an urban complex which included the cities of Portsmouth (west), Chesapeake (south), Virginia Beach (east) and, northward across the harbor of Hampton Roads, Newport News and Hampton.

In the late winter of 1943 I arrived in Norfolk by bus with orders to become part of a large ship's pool, a reserve principally maintained to fill vacancies aboard all kinds of naval vessels on the Atlantic seaboard. As my bus drove through the center of the city, I suddenly observed a drunken sailor being tossed through the plate glass window of a local bar. Nearby was another inebriated sailor in a torn uniform oblivious to the violence that had occurred. He was leaning unsteadily against a lamp post and retching into the gutter. So this was Norfolk!

Well in advance of my arrival I heard many unfavorable tales about Norfolk. It was common knowledge that sailors hated Norfolk. They frequently referred to it as "Shit City," and I quickly learned why. Norfolk was crowded with navy personnel with no place to go. To compound the felony, the civilians disliked the sailors and the sailors in turn disliked the civilians. A story which illustrated this mutual distrust involved a little old lady who boarded a trolley in downtown Norfolk. As usual, it was packed with noisy, unruly sailors. There were no seats. Unexpectedly, a young sailor rose and politely offered his seat to the little old lady. She was so surprised at his genteel behavior that she promptly fainted. When she came to, she thanked the sailor. Then he fainted.

I was immediately assigned to a large unit filled with endless rows of Quonset huts. This immense staging area held several thousand blue jackets all waiting for assignments to ships. My orders called for sea duty on a vessel which used my specialty, sonar. Ships larger than a destroyer would be ruled out. Amphibious duty on various landing craft (such as LSTs, LCIs, and the like) was also excluded.

On the second night after my arrival, shortly after twelve o'clock, a boatswain's mate suddenly entered our Quonset hut ordering us to muster outside on the double. Men in nearby Quonset huts were given the same order. As we stood at attention half-asleep and partially dressed, the reason for this abrupt muster became apparent. Earlier that evening a Navy Wave was allegedly raped and the assailant was presumably in our vicinity. A search was being conducted at once. Moments later, as we stood at attention, down the line came an officer and a chief boatswain escorting a Wave who was weeping. As they passed slowly by, the chief boatswain shined a flashlight in the face of each blue jacket so that the Wave might identify the guilty one. After this inspection party slowly moved on, we were promptly dismissed. To this day I don't know if the rapist was ever caught, but I clearly remember the eyeball to eyeball inspection in the middle of the night. Our hut worried that she could have made a false accusation.

There were thousands of men waiting for assignments in Norfolk. While there, the navy had to keep them busy. In theory, a busy sailor was a happy sailor! Our daily routine never changed. Every morning I mustered under the watchful eyes of several chief boatswains. After the morning roll call, those who wished to visit sick bay for medical reasons were asked to fall out. They were promptly marched away as a separate unit. The rest of us were divided up into small groups and assigned menial tasks which were always servile and lacked dignity. There were no volunteers for these jobs.

I scraped and painted innumerable barracks, rode the back end of garbage trucks, endlessly washed metal trays in the galley, cleaned heads, and for several days dug latrines. One early morning five of us were bused to the local baseball park which had a seating capacity of more than five thousand. There had been a game the previous night and our task was to pick up litter between the seats. Each of us was given a large burlap bag and a wooden stick with a nail on the end and told to go to work. At this point in my life I was losing my identity as a human being. I was quickly becoming a number. I was slowly but surely being committed to eternal serfdom.

Finally, after several weeks of this bleak duty, I gradually learned how to avoid these unpleasant tasks. To my delight, I discovered that once I was outside the assigned work area, but within the base itself, I could move about, look busy, and get lost because of the immensity of the base. It was customary to have all ID cards retained by the officer of the deck. They were released to us only at time of liberty. An ID card was always a pass to freedom. Somehow I came upon a second ID card which was originally issued when I was in the reserve at Wesleyan. It had never been turned in. Thus, I used the extra ID card to escape from my unit. Once outside I spent my daylight hours looking busy and constantly moving. I rode navy buses almost every day traveling the length and width of this immense base with occasional stops for lunch at various PX stores. In time I was worried that the bus drivers would recognize me. One driver, who thought I looked familiar, winked at me one day and said with a big smile, "Hey, Mac, you sure as hell do a lot of traveling around this base." In short, I was "goldbricking" and enjoying every minute of it.

While on liberty in Norfolk we relied on trolleys as our sole means of transportation. Traveling beyond Norfolk to Williamsburg or Washington was virtually impossible, because bus transportation was scarce and our passes from the base had time limits. Every enlisted man's objective was a trip to Washington where women outnumbered men by at least five or six to one. To the lonely sailor, these were intriguing odds. In our barrack we

Dangerous Seas

constantly fantasized about being overwhelmed by beautiful Washington women. But unfortunately Washington was beyond our reach.

One day I heard about two enlisted men who started an illegal round-trip bus ride to Washington. Somehow these two hucksters managed to commandeer a navy bus every weekend and charge handsomely for reserve seats. Enlisted men were so eager to reach Washington, weekend reservations were made well in advance. In time this round trip became so popular, a waiting list developed. Overjoyed with their immediate financial success, these two zealous capitalists expanded their illegal bus service to two, three, and then four navy buses before the authorities caught on. Then the roof fell in. Just before I was transferred to the Charlestown Navy Yard in Boston, I learned that these culprits were given lengthy sentences in a local brig for their daring scheme. I never did get a chance to visit Washington.

While stationed in Norfolk, I often fled the city by taking a ferry to Portsmouth, Virginia where I was an habitual visitor at a local USO, a lively center offering enlisted men all sorts of free entertainment. With a seaman's pay of only $66.00 per month, I had no options. On Saturday nights the USO would sponsor a dance for enlisted personnel. This event usually included a local jazz band, and the surrounding communities would provide well-chaperoned southern girls who came for dancing only. USO regulations clearly stated that under no circumstances could a serviceman date any of the girls. Notwithstanding these restrictions, these dances were mobbed by enlisted men.

The stag line of sailors was three and four feet deep, and men outnumbered women by at least seven or eight to one.

One evening, as a regular customer of the stag line, I gathered sufficient courage to introduce myself to a vivacious, petite blond girl who stood no higher than five feet four inches. She had a beguiling smile, deep blue eyes, and she loved to dance. Her southern accent was captivating, especially for a Yankee lad. Every dance that I had that evening was a moment of joy. During the last dance she told me her name was Jean Markum. As the possessive chaperones were herding their girls into buses, her parting remark was, "I hope to see you next Saturday." Then she was gone. As I took the ferry and trolley back to the base late that evening, I couldn't stop thinking about this beautiful southern belle.

When the next Saturday arrived, I returned to Portsmouth. Jean and I met again on the dance floor. Once more we danced the hours away. I found her to be as radiant and beautiful as ever. I was totally captivated by her. And when the evening ended, she somehow missed the bus, intentionally or otherwise, so I quickly offered to escort her home. She gave me a coy smile and accepted my offer. I was thunderstruck by this unexpected good luck. She was my first real date since entering boot camp some months ago.

I was euphoric!

We boarded the next trolley for the suburbs of Portsmouth and her home. As the trolley came closer to where she lived, I noticed a gradual change in her behavior and conversation. She appeared more reserved and tense. When the trolley reached her neighborhood, she pulled down on the overhead cord alerting the conductor to stop at the next block. The trolley came to a halt, and we both got off. The trolley then continued on its way and slowly disappeared into the darkness. We were at last alone – at which point she stopped abruptly and said, "Home is a block away, and I must walk the rest of the way alone. You must understand that my father waits up for me, hates sailors, and can be quite violent." With that startling announcement, she gave me a quick kiss on the cheek, turned on her heel, and vanished into the night. Alarmed by her remarks, I reluctantly boarded the next trolley and ferry for my long trip back to the base. The next day I received orders to report to Boston for a ship assignment. My romance abruptly ended. I never saw or heard from Jean Markum again.

Dangerous Seas

Boston

In the late spring of 1944, I arrived in Boston and was assigned to the Fargo Building, a navy personnel center providing crews for the Atlantic Fleet. As a liberty town Boston was a great improvement over Norfolk. It had many attractions. Servicemen were well treated. They were given free tickets to concerts, Broadway musicals, the theatre, and Red Sox baseball games. There were many fine restaurants, and the USOs held frequent dances where stage and screen stars frequently acted as hosts. Each night the "Old Howard," a well-known strip joint in Scollay Square, offered visiting sailors their famous striptease acts. Featured performances included "Trixie, the Boa Queen," and ''Bubbles and her Balloon Dance.'' Even the most famous of all strippers, Sally Rand, made an occasional appearance before an overflow crowd of excited, appreciative sailors. In short, Boston offered a variety of entertainment and culture. And for those that looked for it, Boston also offered the seamy side of life.

I used to share liberty with an enlisted man named Fred Schenck from Laguna Beach, California. Fred was unique in many ways. He was handsome, dark-haired, only five feet four, and a mischievous extrovert. He was invariably optimistic and had an engaging laugh. Fred always had within him a boyish sense of fun. He loved to gain attention by acting up in public. What he lacked in height was offset by his wild, outgoing sense of humor and numerous pranks. In civilian life Fred claimed to be Mickey Rooney's stand-in. One evening five of us were having dinner in a well-known, formal restaurant. The occupied tables around us were filled with a clientele known for good breeding and gentility. The maitre d' had a foreign accent, wore white gloves, had impeccable manners, and bowed formally but unctuously to the needs of his dinner guests. I could tell sailors were out of place in this rarefied atmosphere. Moreover, the maitre d' arrogantly assigned us to a small table nearest the kitchen.

This was too much for Fred. When we finished our meal, Fred asked for the check. In the presence of the maitre d' he reviewed the bill for a moment or two. Then he rose from the table and pointed dramatically and repeatedly to the final charge. He shouted it out before a shocked and hushed dining room. As a finale to his dramatic performance, he let go with an earsplitting scream; and to the dismay of the maitre d' and the laughter of his shipmates, he tumbled dramatically to floor in a dead faint. We paid the bill and made a hasty retreat. It was an eventful evening.

Those of us who had liberty with Fred Schenck were always prepared for his histrionics in public. One night following dinner in a large restaurant, he asked for the check. Once again he studied the charges with loud, theatrical comments. And then to the amusement of his shipmates and the surrounding patrons, he poured catsup on the bill and promptly ate it with the balance of his meal.

Being confined to the Fargo Building in downtown Boston and waiting endlessly for sea duty became tedious. Permission to leave the base was granted every other weekend. I soon learned from fellow occupants that security on the base was lax. Many of the personnel were leaving every weekend, unbeknownst to authorities. Since my parents were summering on Cape Cod, I decided I would depart illegally for the Cape on a Friday morning and return on Sunday no later than midnight. Bed checks, I found, were never taken on weekends. The system worked as follows: All ID cards were retained in a yeoman's office and issued only to those who qualified for a weekend pass. In effect, the navy divided personnel into starboard and port passes. ID cards would be issued to port one weekend and to starboard the next. I chose to visit Cape Cod on an unauthorized weekend. One Friday afternoon I decided to leave and involved two friends as part of my scheme. They would pass through the main gate showing their ID cards to the shore patrol. Once outside, one friend returned with two ID cards. He would give me one and I would then pass through the guarded gate. Fortunately, the shore patrol didn't have time to match the picture on the ID Card with the holder hurrying by the main gate.

Three of us planned to meet outside the main gate on Sunday evening and reverse the procedure. I hitchhiked to South Yarmouth on Cape Cod to visit my parents. They were unaware that I was AWOL. Late that Sunday afternoon I successfully hitchhiked back to Boston and waited outside the Fargo Building's main gate for our rendezvous. One hour passed, then another, and no friends. The midnight deadline was fast approaching. In desperation I had to look for other ways of reentering the main gate guarded by the shore patrol. I began to solicit every returning sailor, asking that once inside he return with two ID cards so I could reenter. Obviously, no one wanted to be a party to my crime.

Finally, after hours of soliciting and within a few minutes before twelve, I came upon a good Samaritan. Once inside, he agreed to place his ID card in a package of cigarettes. He promptly appeared in a second story window and tossed the cigarette pack into my waiting hands. Within seconds I successfully passed through the guarded gate, returned the ID card to its owner, and thanked my accomplice profusely for his generous cooperation. Inadvertently I had endangered him as well as myself. In retrospect I learned my lesson. I never went AWOL again.

Dangerous Seas

USS Thomas E. Fraser, DM-24

At morning muster in the Fargo Building, a chief yeoman announced the daily ship assignments, and in early July I finally received orders to report at once to the Charlestown Navy Yard for eventual sea duty. I packed my bag, bade farewell to the Fargo Building, and boarded a navy bus for the harbor. Upon my arrival I saw my new home for the next sixteen months and eighteen days. Tied to a nearby pier was the *Thomas E. Fraser*, a new, sleek destroyer with the most graceful lines I've ever seen. She was adorned in her new camouflage colors of the Atlantic Fleet. She was a beautiful vessel designed principally for speed, and I thought of John Paul Jones' famous statement, "Give me a fast ship, for I intend to go in harm's way." At that time I was unaware of how prophetic these famous words would become.

I mounted the gangway at once, saluted the colors on the stern, and then the officer of the deck, requesting, "Permission to come aboard, sir." Once I was logged in as a member of the crew, I went aft to the crew's quarters located below the after deck where I stowed my gear in a small, metal foot locker. Directly above were three tiers of canvas bunks. Each bunk was lashed with line to a folding metal frame. When not in use, the bunks folded up against the bulkhead to provide additional space. With a beam of only forty feet, a destroyer, I found, had little room. Every inch of space had to be utilized. I was assigned to the top bunk and I couldn't sit up without striking my head against pipes and wires that ran along the overhead not more than twenty-four inches above my sack.

The *Thomas E. Fraser*, originally DD 736, was built in Bath, Maine in the spring of 1944. A skeleton crew sailed her to Boston for conversion from destroyer to destroyer minelayer. Her torpedo tubes were removed and replaced with mine tracks running topside down the port and starboard sides of the main and after decks. In addition, she was outfitted with greater antiaircraft fire power. The *Fraser* was one of twelve ships undergoing this conversion. At the time of conversion our squadron was designed to race at high speed to an enemy harbor and drop mines, thereby sealing off enemy ships. However, by the time our squadron reached the Pacific, the once proud Japanese Fleet was no longer a threat to our navy. Hence, our duties would include air protection for our mine craft sweeping mine fields before invasions. We would follow our "sweeps" off the beaches, dropping buoys to identify areas cleared of mines. We would also be involved in convoying, antisubmarine patrols, shore bombardment, and radar picket duty.

On August 23, 1944, our ship was commissioned in the Charlestown Navy Yard. She was named after Commander Thomas E. Fraser, who went down on his destroyer, the *Walke*, in the battle of the Coral Sea in 1942. In command of our ship was Commander Ronald J. Woodaman, an Annapolis graduate, Class of 1931. Woodaman already had extensive sea duty. He served aboard the destroyer *USS O'Brien* in Iceland and the North Atlantic. He had command of the destroyer *Bensen (DD 421)* in the Mediterranean where he received the Silver Star, the Bronze Medal, the Navy Commendation Medal, and the Purple Heart. He was a seasoned destroyer veteran.

Our executive officer was Lieutenant Commander William Ingram, also an Annapolis graduate, whose father, Admiral Jonas Ingram, was in command of the Atlantic Sea Frontier. Bill Ingram was a husky, amiable man who had been a football star at Annapolis. He was also very popular with the crew. When the Japs bombed Pearl Harbor on December 7th, Ingram saw action aboard a battleship on Battleship Row. (Ingram would eventually leave our ship to become skipper of *USS Shannon*, a member of our squadron.)

Our ship's company consisted of 22 officers and approximately 376 men. Our crew were largely reservists from civilian life: postal clerks, machinists, farmers, railroad engineers, riveters, bricklayers, plumbers, and salesmen. Geographically, most of the crew came from the south and had no prior sea duty.

The Fraser's armaments consisted of six 5-inch/38 caliber guns, ten 20mm and twelve 40mm antiaircraft batteries. She had a designed top speed of 34 knots and was driven by two geared turbine engines. Her fuel capacity was 500 tons, and her maximum cruising range was 5,010 miles at 15.8 knots.

Heading up our sonar group was Ensign David Jones, a Yale alumnus, Class of 1945. He was recently commissioned, had never been to sea, and was initially nervous about his new seafaring responsibilities. He was slight in stature and appeared young for his age. Yet he was very conscientious, learned his job quickly, and soon gained the respect of his men. Because of his size and youth, the captain at times would bully Jones in our presence when we were at general quarters or on watch. The sonar gang silently shared Jones's anguish and felt that the captain's actions were uncalled for.

John O'Connor, sonarman first class, was our senior enlisted man. He joined the navy right out of high school and intended to make it his career. While on the *Fraser*, he made chief sonarman. (After the war he stayed in the navy, moved up through the ranks, and retired as a captain.) O'Connor was a rough-cut, self-educated man knowledgeable about sonar. He was a good petty officer, had a ready sense of humor and took great pride in his Irish heritage. He was always telling Irish jokes with the aid of an authentic brogue.

Henry Slivinski, sonarman third class, came from Syracuse, New York. He was a happily married man with five children. In civilian life Henry was a milkman. I felt sorry for him because he missed his family so desperately.

Dangerous Seas

It was a great hardship for him to be in the service. His devoted wife, Wanda, was always sending food packages which Henry shared with us. Known as "Ski," he looked Slavic with his blond hair, high cheek bones, and bright blue eyes. "Ski" was easy going, always had a friendly smile, and we soon became good friends. In moments of relaxation he taught me a few Polish phrases and sentences, which I still remember after more than fifty years. At sea I learned such useful sentences as, "How is everything in the old country?" "Poland is not yet dead." "You are a very pretty girl," and "Kiss my ass!" In the Pacific, I found no one who could speak Polish, so I had no opportunity to display my bilingual talents.

Another member of our sonar group was Pat Peterson, sonarman second class, who came from Galesburg, Illinois. He was a handsome blond in his late twenties who was always talking about women. In preparation for liberty, he would spend hours primping and grooming his hair and patting his face and body with various scented lotions which he thought would make him irresistible to the women he chased. He owned tight fitting tailor-made dress blues with bell-bottom trousers extended at the bottom an extra two inches for style. His white sailor hat was always set forward on his head in a rakish manner exactly two fingers above his eyebrows. In the navy we called his style "salty."

Peterson would frequently share liberty with O'Connor, who also was on the prowl for women. When they returned from their adventurous escapades, our sonar group would frequently gather and listen intently to their tales of conquests. Those of us not skilled in the art of meeting voluptuous women, marveled at their stories, true or otherwise.

No description of our sonar gang would be complete without mentioning Tom Hansen, seaman second class. Hansen joined our ship's company shortly after the *Fraser* was commissioned. He was in his early forties, married with children, and came from Albany, New York. He was the oldest member of our group and was often called "Pop." In civilian life he was a contented mailman and his only brush with history came from the fact that his daily mail route included deliveries to the home of Governor Thomas E. Dewey. As a sailor, "Pop" Hansen was a total misfit. He was overweight, had poor eyesight, and was flatfooted. Additionally, every time we had trial sea runs out of Boston Harbor, Hansen became violently seasick. In fact, if he heard the anchor chain rising, he claimed he was ill. When we left for our six-week shakedown cruise to Bermuda, poor Hansen was continuously nauseated. He spent the entire trip in his sack or hanging over the rail without his false teeth. At sick bay one morning, a pharmacist's mate, lacking sympathy for his condition, said to him, "What you need is a big glass of machine oil." At that statement, Hansen began to vomit. When we returned to Norfolk following our Bermuda shakedown, "Pop" Hansen was given instant shore duty. Subsequently rumors circulated that he eventually was medically discharged. We all wondered if he was back in Albany on his old mail route delivering mail to Governor Thomas E. Dewey. We never found out because we never heard of or saw him again. The last member of our sonar group was "Gibby" Gibson, seaman first class, who originally hailed from the hills of Tennessee. As a boy, he joined Ringling Brothers Circus in Sarasota, Florida where he became an elephant trainer. "Gibby" stood no higher than 5' 4" and developed a pot from overeating and drinking beer. He was a heavy smoker and his teeth were yellow from tobacco stains. At sea he grew a full beard, and in the evenings he frequently sang hillbilly songs while he played his guitar. He was an authority on circus life and regaled us with laughter about life under the big tent. He lectured us on the differences between the African and Indian elephant. (The African elephant is larger and has bigger ears). To the amusement of his audience, he also held symposiums on the sex life of an elephant. For example, we learned that the male elephant has no scrotum, the testes being retained inside. We found his frequent dissertations entertaining and educational. "Gibby" had every expectation of returning to circus life after the war.

Dangerous Seas

Bermuda

After the commissioning of the *Fraser*, we remained in port tied alongside other destroyers. Ship fitters, welders, electricians, and other sailors swarmed over our ship night and day to ready her for sea duty. The constant clatter and hammering of riveters, especially at night, made it difficult to sleep. On September 25th, we made the first of our many trial runs out of Boston. We frequently sailed by Provincetown where our quartermasters took bearings from one of Cape Cod's familiar landmarks, Pilgrim's Monument. Seeing this towering structure rising majestically at the tip of the Cape was always a nostalgic sight for me. As a boy, I climbed to its top many times.

At least two-thirds of our crew were inexperienced and had never been to sea. But we gradually acquired skills through never-ending drills: boarding and salvage parties, armed boat party drills, fire and rescue, abandon ship drills, and speed trials going to general quarters. Training exercises at sea were conducted at the turn of the season when New England's early frost and crisp winds gave a tang to the air, signifying the arrival of fall.

On October 4, 1944, we received orders to sail to Bermuda for our shakedown cruise in the company of three ships in our squadron, the *Smith* (DM 23), the *Shannon (DM 25)*, and the *Bauer (DM 26)*. Our little flotilla of destroyer minelayers (designated Mine Division 7) entered the Atlantic and began a zigzag course south. At dusk, when we went to general quarters, we received our first alert. A German U-boat had torpedoed a cargo ship off Cape Hatteras the night before. Shipmates who had prior experience on the Atlantic, expressed great respect for German submarines. That evening I had my first watch on the sonar gear (first watch 8:00 p.m. to midnight). Because of the sub alert, I was especially mindful of my responsibilities for the safety of our ship.

The second day at sea a severe storm caught us off Cape Hatteras. Our three ships pitched and rolled in mountainous waves. At times our bow plowed under oncoming seas causing icy ocean sprays to cover the prow of our ship and bridge. Some of the crew were seasick and heaving over the rail was a common sight. This act was known as "feeding the fish." Fortunately I wasn't ill, but I had no appetite for meals that day.

On October 6th, we reached the warm and welcome waters of Bermuda without incident. We entered Hamilton Harbor immediately for assignment. Since Bermuda was a major embarkation port for Europe, the anchorage was crowded with destroyers, light cruisers, destroyer escorts, minesweepers, Canadian corvettes, destroyer tenders, fuel tankers, transports, and cargo vessels. Hamilton Harbor was so jammed with ships coming and going, we had to anchor several miles from the docks. No shore leave was given because we began an intensified training program. We commenced daily antisubmarine exercises with *USS Grady (DE 445)*, *USS Bath (PF 55)*, *USS Hank (DD 702)*, *USS Bauer (DM26)*, *USS Shannon (DM 25)*, *USS Smith (DM 23)*, *USS Lind (DD 703)* and *USS Borie (DD 704)*. Each day our "war games" involved tracking "tame" World War I German and Italian submarines. These old subs, manned by American crews, tried to evade our sonar searches, and if we made underwater contact, we fired dummy hedgehogs. We had trouble tracking the Italian submarine *Da Prosida*. On a moment's notice she could reverse her propellers and move backwards at high speed. This odd maneuver would invariably confuse our sonar operators and permit the sub to escape.

One bright and sunny day, while performing antisub drills with "tame" submarines, a World War II German submarine somehow managed to approach our little task force unnoticed. All hell broke loose when she fired a live torpedo across the bow of a nearby destroyer escort. This unexpected incident drove our flotilla into total chaos. We had to surface all of our "tame" subs before we could search for the "live" submarine. Once our submarines had surfaced, we searched in vain for the German U-boat. We never found her.

As weeks passed, our routine at sea remained the same. We continued with antisubmarine runs, held damage control exercises, smoke drills, man overboard, abandon ship, and antiaircraft maneuvers. We fired at drone planes and towed sleeves with our 20mm, 40mm and 5-inch mounts. My battle station was above the bridge and just aft of our forward twin 5-inch guns. The noise of these explosions was not only deafening, but each five-inch salvo would shake the hull of our ship. Moreover, the thunder from our guns was coupled with the noise of empty shell cases clattering across the ship's metal decks.

One afternoon during antisubmarine maneuvers, the destroyer *Lind (DD 603)* inadvertently fired a dummy torpedo which passed harmlessly under our hull. Our captain was enraged over this incident. He immediately used the ship's radio to chew out the skipper of the *Lind* with an endless flow of profanity.

After four weeks of lengthy maneuvers, the *Fraser* remained at anchor in Hamilton Harbor. The captain decided to give ship's company their first liberty. Navy launches arrived in the morning to bring us to Hamilton. Once ashore, most of the crew headed straight to the nearest bars where they drank heavily until departure time. At five o'clock, when liberty ended, I was on the last departing launch headed for the *Fraser*. The hold of our ship was crammed with drunken sailors. Some had passed out, others were vomiting over the launch's gunwales, and a few lay motionless with torn, bloody uniforms. The launch was so crowded with drunks that I had to stand on the fantail next to the coxswain. From my vantage point I looked down into the

Dangerous Seas

hold and saw a writhing, distorted jumble of youthful sailors. The scene reminded me of freshly unearthed, twisting earth worms following a rain storm.

When the launch finally reached the *Fraser*, I watched inebriated sailors climb aboard from a pitching boat up the ship's narrow, swaying ladder to safety. There were some trying moments, but everyone came aboard without any serious injuries.

Although our brief visit to Bermuda occurred during the war years, in memory's eye it was and always will be one of my favorite regions of the earth. With its soft colors of white, pale blue, and pinks, this island was surrounded by the beauty and mystery of a sparkling, undulating sea, an exhalation of radiant colors. In my idle moments off watch, I often observed with fascination the ocean's spray rising off the windward bows of ships journeying to unknown destinations. At dusk, while at general quarters, I frequently watched the afternoon sun sink slowly beneath the sea. And the nights that followed brought forth a galaxy of brilliant stars whose light illuminated dark and lonesome skies. I wondered if I would ever get home again. I thought about my father's nostalgic statement, "There is a mystical healing quality for those who are on the sea."

On November 3, 1944, the *Thomas E. Fraser* received orders to proceed to Norfolk for final repairs and outfitting. As we weighed anchor and reluctantly sailed north from Bermuda, we received notice that our ship was being assigned to the Pacific Fleet. I viewed this transfer with some concern, for the Pacific was so vast and limitless.

I would be farther from home than ever.

Dangerous Seas

Assignment to the Pacific

The *Fraser* returned to Norfolk on November 3, 1944. It was a great disappointment that Boston would no longer be our home port. For the next three weeks our ship underwent routine repairs. There wasn't time for liberty, but I wasn't that anxious to revisit the city of Norfolk. Each day we made daily trips to nearby Bloodworth Island where we, along with other destroyer minelayers, conducted daytime mine-laying exercises and shore bombardment. And at night we illuminated the landscape with star shells, a practice we would soon follow to prevent infiltration by Japs.

On the cold, brisk morning of November 22, 1944 our winches slowly raised our two anchors while deckhands hosed off mud collected on the anchor chains. Concurrently the ensign on the bow was lowered to signify that the ship was underway. Immediately, the shrill whistle of a boatswain's pipe came over the P.A. system with the familiar words, "Now hear this! The smoking lamp is out. Sweepers, man your brooms. Clean sweep down fore and aft." The *Fraser* headed into the open sea. Her sharp bow knifed through the rolling blue-green waves, and once again we were sailing the stormy Atlantic.

Three ships, *Shannon (DM 25), Bauer (DM 26),* and *Fraser (DM 24),* had orders to convoy the cruiser *Alaska* to Guantanamo Bay, Cuba. The *Alaska* was a beautiful ship of battleship size with lean cruiser lines. She was a recent member of the fleet, having been commissioned as recently as June 1944. This 27,500-ton warship had a main battery of nine 12-inch guns and twelve 5-inch antiaircraft guns. She was 808 feet long, could travel at better than 30 knots, and had a ship's company of approximately 1500 men.

After spending only a day at Guantanamo Bay, our little task force headed south for the tropical waters of Panama. Upon arrival, we immediately entered the locks of the Canal, tied to the *Bauer*. It took the better part of a day to reach the Pacific. En route, I recall watching beautiful, tropical birds in the nearby jungle bordering both sides of the ship. There were no sea breezes, and the tropical heat was stifling.

Journeying across the isthmus of Panama was a trip of about 50 miles through a series of locks and lakes. On the way our ship stopped at Colon, a primitive and unhealthy settlement largely populated by blacks originating from the British West Indies. The ancestors of the present population were originally imported at the turn of the century to perform manual labor when the Canal was first constructed. This desolate and decaying town was a liberty port for blue jackets en route to the Pacific. All liberty parties going ashore were warned that this location was rampant with sexually transmitted diseases, syphilis, gonorrhea, and crab lice.

To compound the felony, I was assigned shore patrol duty that evening and my beat included the red-light district. My uniform was a black armband with bright yellow initials, "S. P." I was equipped with a police whistle and a heavy, wooden billy club. Our assignment that evening was a row of decadent, broken-down bars filled with drunken sailors and hard-looking women pursuing the Yankee dollar. For safety, we patrolled on foot in twos. The evening had its share of excitement. We broke up bar fights, stopped a mugging, and tossed several inebriated blue jackets into roving paddy wagons.

The red-light district was located on a narrow, unlit dirt road lined with one or two-room dilapidated shacks on stilts. Seated on the front steps of each shanty were bedraggled, unsightly women. In strident voices, each solicited passing sailors in Spanish or broken English. Since there was a midnight curfew, I had the added responsibility of evicting several patrons from these houses of ill repute. At midnight a tropical rain storm began at the same time we had to eject patrons from these shacks. In doing so, the shore patrol incurred the wrath of drenched sailors and their women. I finally returned to the ship in the early morning hours, fatigued but comforted by the fact that my assignment was over. Luckily, I never had shore patrol duty again.

On December 4, 1944, the *Shannon*, *Bauer*, *Fraser*, and *Alaska* entered the wide Pacific. Our destination was San Diego. As we sailed northward up the coast of Central America, to the east in the distance I could see the mountainous terrain of Honduras, Guatemala, and Mexico. Our trip from Panama to San Diego was a journey of about 2800 miles. Along the way we conducted daily exercises: abandon ship, fire drills, laying smoke screens, and antiaircraft practice. During one of these exercises, a plane from the *Alaska* crashed into the sea. The *Bauer* was immediately sent to the scene of the accident. Fortunately, the pilot and the plane were rescued.

One late afternoon while standing watch on the sonar gear, I picked up unusual underwater sounds which did not sound like a submarine, yet we were closing in on a distinct moving target off our starboard bow. I notified the bridge. "Bridge, this is sonar. We have a sonar contact bearing 010 degrees, 1,000 yards and closing." The captain decided it was serious enough to sound general quarters. Immediately over the P.A. system came the familiar call, "All Hands, man your battle stations." Within a few seconds I was relieved from my post so that I could go to my battle station above the bridge. All eyes anxiously strained ahead to identify the contact. The tension was soon broken when a lookout identified our contact as a pod of whales. Because of the false alarm, the sonarmen received a good razzing from our shipmates.

Living at sea for a long period of time with 376 men on a vessel 376 feet long presented problems in human relations. It gradually became known among the crew that I had two years of college under my belt. In those days, particularly in the navy, an enlisted man with a college education was a rarity. In addition, I had the luxury of attending one of the finest preparatory schools in the country, Deerfield Academy. My father, a college professor, was not a wealthy man, but he knew educators, the best schools, and the importance of having a good education. As a result, I was lucky to have a scholarship. In contrast, only a few of my peers on the *Fraser* had completed high school. Because of my educational background, perhaps I was overly conscious of this difference. I sensed an element of initial suspicion among my shipmates.

Class distinction was prevalent in the navy. Career officers, all of whom were Annapolis graduates, naturally had more responsible jobs and tended to socialize with other Annapolis graduates. On the other hand, reserve officers were looked upon as "90 day wonders" by some Annapolis men and career enlisted men. Among members of the crew there was also a distinction between "regular navy" and civilians who enlisted or were drafted for the duration of the war. Aboard our ship there were differences which I tried to treat with humor. Enlisted men stood in line with metal trays for cafeteria-style meals served in a crowded mess hall, while officers were served different and better meals in the ward room tended by blacks and Philippino waiters.

Another oddity, which amused me, was the frequent P.A. announcement, "Now hear this. Air officers' bedding, air officers' bedding," whereupon the black and Philippine culinary staff would dutifully place officers' mattresses on guard rails for their periodic airing. To my knowledge, the bedding in the crowded crew's quarters never received this preferential treatment.

At sea aboard a destroyer in wartime, I found a bluejacket's daily tasks never ending. To run a successful warship required the experience and skill of many hands. Each division had its share of responsibilities. One of the most respected tasks in the navy was the duty of the quartermaster. His domain was the bridge and the pilot house. His job, among other duties, involved navigation. He assisted the navigation officer in charting the ship's course. He also kept records, the ship's log, and continuously kept an eye on weather reports. At battle stations, a quartermaster was located at the after steering station, ready to assume the wheel if the pilot house suffered damage during combat.

Every ship had signalmen who were located on the flying bridge. It was their responsibility to provide visual communication between ships traveling in a convoy when radio silence was maintained. Visual communication was accomplished in one of three ways: by signal searchlight using Morse code, by flag hoist, and by waving semaphore flags. Signalmen were often called "flags" by the crew.

During the months I served aboard the *Fraser*, I never once ventured into the engine rooms below deck. To get there, one had to pass through a small hatchway and carefully descend down a metal ladder into the bowels of the ship. Here, men stood watches in a world surrounded by heat, pumps, motors, and constant noise. Below deck the *Fraser* had two engine rooms. Firemen maintained roaring oil fires that heated four large boilers in two fire rooms. The heated water in the boilers converted to steam which, in turn, passed through and turned the ship's large turbines moving the ship to a maximum speed of 33 or 34 knots.

During combat the men below deck were secured in water tight compartments; their only communication with the outside world was by telephone. If a ship was hit in battle by bombs or shell fire, there was always the hazard of oil fires, the release of hot steam, or the flooding of a compartment by sea water. In the event a vessel was mortally wounded and "abandon ship" was ordered, men below deck were frequently unable to escape. They were often trapped and went down with the ship.

Similarly, gunners' mates also had hazardous duty. Each twin five-inch mount required at least a dozen men in the magazine, handling room, and gun room, all below deck. During general quarters, these men were ready to start projectiles and powder cases up electrical hoists. Topside our twin forties, two quad forties, and 20mm gun crews were totally unprotected, except for small splinter shields. Enemy gunfire or a kamikaze hit took its toll of these topside sailors.

On a Sumner Class destroyer, such as the *Fraser*, we had no hospital beds or isolation wards. The medical officer, usually a lieutenant senior grade, and two pharmacist mates dispensed medical aid from a tiny cubicle located amidships on the port side. Elsewhere throughout the ship were bags and boxes of dressings, antiburn solutions, disinfectants, penicillin, morphine syrettes, and other medical supplies strategically placed about the vessel, including life rafts. During my months at sea, morphine syrettes from our life rafts would periodically disappear. Notwithstanding the many attempts to identify the thief, the culprit was never exposed or caught.

In addition, our ship was well supplied with yeomen, storekeepers, electricians, fire controlmen, metal smiths, radar technicians, and boatswains. Finally, there was the continuous battle against rust. Daily, work parties of seamen roamed the ship in an endless chipping detail scraping rust from the decks and superstructure. This chore was always the same. First, the rust was chipped away. Then a primer of yellow paint was applied, followed by a final coat of battleship grey.

Dangerous Seas

Pearl Harbor

On December 12, 1944, our task force reached San Diego. From there to December 19th, we conducted extensive maneuvers off San Clemente Island. On December 20th, we set sail for Pearl Harbor. Accompanied by destroyers *Shannon* and *Bauer*, we convoyed two army transports, *USS General E.T. Callon* and the *USS E.C. Collins*. Aboard these two transports were army personnel and a large number of army nurses. As we proceeded westward on a zigzag course, our lookouts on the bridge spent more time watching the nurses with binoculars than scanning the seas for periscopes and floating mines.

As our convoy headed westward, the shores of San Diego and southern California slowly faded in the mist. I realized that I was now more than 3,000 miles from home. I wondered when, if ever, I would see the United States again. For me, Christmas day, December 25, 1944, was not a traditional holiday. I was alone at sea and away from my home and family. My only reminder of this holy day was a Christmas tree hoisted to the yardarm of the *General Collins*, and for lunch our captain ordered a turkey dinner for the crew.

The next day the weather cleared and we got our first glimpse of beautiful Hawaii. Our little convoy sailed around famous Diamond Head and slowly passed through the narrow entrance of Pearl Harbor. We passed Battleship Row and Ford Island where I observed the remnants of the sunken battleships, *Arizona* and *Oklahoma*. It was only three years earlier that the Japanese executed their sneak attack on Pearl Harbor.

Some scars from the bombing remained. Nevertheless, inside the harbor, ships were everywhere, battleships, cruisers, destroyers, destroyer escorts, aircraft carriers, minesweepers, transports, gasoline tankers, destroyer tenders, and various auxiliary vessels. The might of the United States Navy had grown enormously since the days of 1941 and 1942. We eventually dropped anchor at Pearl City, a section in the harbor reserved for destroyers.

For the first time I noticed several badly damaged warships anchored nearby. One vessel had lost its bow, while others had demolished superstructures. The more severely damaged ships would leave for the west coast shipyards. Others would be repaired at Pearl Harbor. In conversations with personnel of these ships, I learned that they had just returned from the Philippine invasion. Most of the damage resulted from conventional air attacks. But the Japanese were now resorting to a new tactic, using suicide planes called "kamikazes" to crash into our ships. In effect, this new strategy had initial successes, because there was simply no defense against this kind of attack. Moreover, the introduction of kamikazes as a weapon struck terror in the hearts of our sailors. In the months ahead I would soon learn more about these suicide tactics.

During my brief stay in Pearl Harbor, I had several unusual experiences. While on liberty, I decided, like most tourists, to visit the famous resort, Waikiki Beach. On arrival I found a small, over-populated beach surrounded by high rise hotels. Servicemen were everywhere. I was very disappointed and left as soon as I could. That afternoon I took a bus to Honolulu and found the city also jammed with navy personnel. To avoid crowds I turned down a side street and encountered a small group of sailors patiently standing in line before a seedy building with a marquee over the entrance. As I came closer, I expected to see a movie house featuring a popular show. Upon closer examination, and to my surprise, it turned out to be a whorehouse.

Although our stay in Hawaii lasted about a month, I never had another shore leave, because there was no time for liberty. The destroyer minelayers of Mine Division Seven, that is, *Fraser*, *Bauer*, *Shannon*, and *Smith*, were too busy at sea on daily trials and maneuvers. The weather was ideal with temperatures in the seventies with ever-present balmy sea breezes. Our sea trials involved more gunnery exercises, firing at drones, shore bombardment with landing craft and simulated troop landings. Additionally, we conducted mine laying and at night we fired endless star shells to illuminate potential enemy infiltrations.

To the familiar call of general quarters both day and night, all hands would immediately race to battle stations. Rushing to battle stations in total darkness on a rolling ship had its anxious moments. Each department would then call the bridge saying, for example, "Sonar manned and ready." In time all departments would report to the bridge in less than three minutes. Through never-ending drills, the *Fraser* was at last rounding into a first-class fighting ship.

On January 26, 1945, we left Pearl Harbor to join a large convoy of destroyers, cruisers and troop transports loaded with marines. Our task force headed west passing more damaged warships, including the cruiser *Quincy*. She was also returning from the Philippine invasion. Once again, most of the damage to these vessels was caused by Jap suicide planes. It now became increasingly apparent that we would join an invasion force somewhere in the vast Pacific. Navy scuttlebutt suggested that we might be part of a proposed landing force in the Bonin Islands, north of Iwo Jima, and only a few hundred miles south of Japan. We awaited our unknown destination with excitement and apprehension.

Dangerous Seas

Iwo Jima

On February 9, 1945, the *Fraser*, along with the destroyer *Guest*, departed Enewetok at dawn convoying the Battleship *New York*, one of the oldest warships of the fleet. Because of her age, the *New York* could no longer travel in a fast-moving carrier group. She had become one of the "old ladies" of the fleet. She could always be identified by her old-fashion tripod mast. Her lack of speed, mobility, and antiaircraft firepower limited her wartime duties to shore bombardment. Battleships would soon become relics of the past.

Two days later, on February 11th, our small flotilla reached Saipan in the Marianas. Nearby were the islands of Tinian and Guam, now under United States control. Large airfields were now operational for our B-29 bombers. We saw their formations leaving daily on bombing missions over Japan. They were enormous planes and, according to intelligence reports, were very effective in destroying Japan's war efforts. The next day at anchor, the crew spent the day loading ammunition and supplies for our undertaking, the invasion of Iwo Jima in the Volcano Islands north of Saipan.

On February 16th, two immense task forces, Group A, Task Group 51.11, and Group B. Task Group 51.12 sailed from Saipan. Nearly 500 ships made up our armada, including 200 attack transports carrying marines of the Third, Fourth, and Fifth Divisions. Also in our convoy were LSTs, supply ships, tankers with 10,000,000 gallons of fuel, two white hospital ships with large red crosses painted on their hulls, fleet oilers, escort carriers, ammunition minesweepers, destroyers, destroyer escorts, and six battleships, the "old ladies" of the fleet, the *Texas*, *New York*, *Tennessee*, *Arkansas*, *Nevada*, and *Idaho*. This was the biggest assemblage of warships that I had seen. I remember thinking that if we were going into battle, there was some comfort in knowing we were not alone.

Once underway, we lined up for tetanus shots and I experienced a brief fainting spell from the serum. In preparation for the invasion all hands were instructed to wear life belts at all times and keep our shirts on with sleeves rolled down to protect our skin from possible fires and powder burns. Our watches were changed from Condition Three to Condition Two. That is, instead of four hours on and eight hours off, we went to four hours on and four hours off. Most watertight doors were dogged closed.

On February 18th, after two days on our northerly course, our huge convoy was spotted by high-flying Japanese reconnaissance planes, which were immediately but unsuccessfully pursued by our combat air patrol. Certainly, our approaching invasion force was no longer a surprise to the enemy. In fact, in the late afternoon that same day, we heard on the radio for the first time the infamous "Tokyo Rose" broadcasting her propaganda from Japan. She predicted an invasion of Iwo Jima and accurately named some of the ships in our invasion force. She also indicated that the Japanese air force had already inflicted widespread damage to many of our vessels. Her soothing and convincing voice, along with her predictions of American losses, raised my anxiety level. I wondered if we were sailing into a trap.

For me, going into combat for the first time brought forth a mood of exhilaration, an appetite for adventure, genuine fear, and esprit de corps. There was also an inward foreboding of death. In retrospect, youths in their twenties simply cannot comprehend their own mortality, yet the shadow of death falls on every man in battle. Certainly the mystery of war shrouds the deeper mystery of death. In war, death lurks everywhere.

For the *Fraser*, D-Day began on February 19, 1945. At three a.m., as we approached Iwo, I heard and eventually saw continued explosions and red flashes on the horizon caused by a fierce naval bombardment from our warships. Off watch some of us gathered in the mess hall to listen to radio reports and "Tokyo Rose" once again. We were anxiously waiting the call to general quarters. To pass the time, one shipmate was playing a hillbilly tune on his guitar. Another was finishing a letter to his wife, while a third member of the crew was deeply absorbed in reading passages from the Bible.

Then, at four o'clock, came the familiar call, "All hands, man your battle stations." In the minutes that followed, the officers and crew of the *Fraser* were prepared for battle. With the arrival of dawn, all eyes strained for the first view of Iwo Jima. The weather was raw, cold, and damp. In the early morning light, I could see in the distance the dormant volcanic cone of Mt. Suribachi rising 550 feet in the air, shrouded in mist and smoke from naval gunfire. From the sea Iwo Jima resembled a barren mass of black, brown, and grey rocks. As we came closer, there appeared to be no trees, and we could smell sulphur, which accounted for Iwo's name. (Iwo Jima in Japanese means "hot rocks.")

From Mt. Suribachi, the island stretched northward about five miles, ending in prominent cliffs overlooking the sea. In short, Iwo Jima had no jungles, no real mountains, no water, and no birds. It resembled an uninhabitable, God-forsaken stone and volcanic ash fortress set far out in the sea.

At the proposed area where our marines would land, navy frog men were quickly dispersed along the shore to determine if there were any mines or underwater barriers blocking the landing area. They found none. Meanwhile, just off the beach, 43 minesweepers moved in to search for moored, magnetic, and acoustic mines. The destroyers *Fraser*, *Shannon*, *Gwin*, and *Lindsey* followed the "sweeps" providing protection against enemy shore batteries located in hillside caves on Mt. Suribachi. Only one mine was located about ten miles east of the island. Enemy small-fire began

Dangerous Seas

and scored some hits, so the cruiser *Pensacola* arrived to provide additional fire power. Within three minutes, she in turn was hit by enemy shore batteries and had to retire. Once the sweeping had been completed, the old battleships of the fleet, the *Texas, New York, Idaho, Arkansas,* and *Tennessee* (built between 1914 and 1917), commenced shelling the beaches with their 74 mounted guns ranging from 12 to 16 inches. It was a murderous barrage. The noise was deafening.

Early that same morning a chaplain on board one of the troop transports distributed to the marines cards containing the words of Sir Jacob Astley before the battle of Edgehill during England's Civil War of 1642. It read, "Oh Lord, Thou knowest how busy I must be on this day: If I forget Thee, do not forget me."

From our patrol station south of the island, I watched marines scramble down nets into amphibious craft. Once aboard, the small landing boats filled with marines circled near the troop transports awaiting word to head for the beach. At approximately 9:00 a.m., the command was given and the countless assault vessels, the first of 75,000 men, headed for the shore. By then the shore bombardment had ceased. As wave after wave of these marines approached the soft, treacherous sands of the island, the Japs were waiting. I wondered how many would survive this bloody ordeal, and how many would face certain death. I was witnessing in awe and admiration the deadly spectacle of marines assaulting the beaches of Iwo Jima. It was a scene I will never forget.

At 2:00 p.m. the Fraser left her submarine patrol station south of the island and moved to within 1,000 yards of Mt. Suribachi to aid in the bombardment. We shelled caves, pill boxes, and other enemy installations targeted for us by marine spotters ashore. This action continued the rest of day, and from sunset until dawn we fired star shells over the southern part of the island to prevent the Japs from infiltrating our lines.

For the next few days we shelled Mt. Suribachi during the daylight hours, fired star shells at night, and in time were relieved by other warships. We would then return to a patrol station to replenish our supply of food, fuel, and ammunition from nearby cargo and ammunition ships. During one bombardment our gunners killed some Japanese swimmers attempting a flank attack behind marine lines.

During these busy times no one slept. Some of us began to get the drawn-cheek, puffy-eyed look of destroyer sailors. At the same time, the cooks would run out of eggs, ham, bacon, meat, and fresh vegetables. Our culinary staff would then turn to beans, Spam, dry cereal, canned fruit, and powdered milk. And at times we survived on K rations. They were always the same, tasteless crackers, tinned meat, a fruit bar, and, if the box was marked "breakfast," toilet paper. After several days of K rations, I remember "Gibby" Gibson, seaman first class and former elephant trainer, grumbling about the food. He said, "Hell, my elephants at Ringling Brothers get better food than this!"

Because of the frequent use of our guns, we had to tie up to an ammunition ship every few days to reload. I hated ammunition detail, for it required hours of hard manual labor. All of us had to carry on our shoulders heavy, greasy five-inch shells from the ammunition ship to our hoists. Each shell must have weighed at least fifty pounds. This task would be repeated endlessly until our magazines were full. My left shoulder always became lame and covered with heavy grease. During this detail I always worried about enemy air raids. One direct hit among all of these explosives would send us all to kingdom come.

During the early days of the Iwo campaign we experienced very little enemy air activity. Perhaps the Japs were preoccupied with the Third Fleet bombing targets on the Japanese mainland. On February 21st, however, circumstances changed. Japanese suicide planes suddenly appeared and attacked the carrier *Bismarck Sea* southwest of the island. From my battle station I could see large explosions and fires on the horizon caused by kamikaze aircraft. A tug arrived to aid the crippled ship, but she sank before any assistance could reach her. We had no word of casualties. About the same time, north of Iwo the carrier *Saratoga* sustained heavy damage from five kamikazes. One hundred and ten of the crew were killed and 80 were badly wounded. The *Saratoga* had to withdraw from Iwo for home to undergo major repairs.

Meanwhile, two marine divisions, the Fourth and Fifth, landed side by side. The Fifth's objective was to cut across the island's narrow neck and seize Mt. Suribachi. The Fourth would swing north to capture the two airfields. The going was very rough and the casualties were staggering. By the end of the first day, 2,420 of the 30,000 marines who landed on D-Day were dead or wounded.

There were 22,000 Japanese soldiers on Iwo Jima under the command of General Tadamichi Kuribayashi, a veteran of the China campaign. Knowing that Iwo would eventually be attacked, his troops had many months to fortify their island. There were approximately 750 major installations built to house guns. Underneath Mt. Suribachi alone was a four-story galley and hospital. Altogether the marines were confronted by 13,000 tunnels and over 5,000 pill boxes and caves. Just prior to the invasion, Kuribayashi, knowing he would never receive reinforcements, wrote to his wife a final letter saying, "Do not plan on my return."

In the interim the *Fraser*, with several other destroyers, continued to shell Mt. Suribachi, as the marines slowly moved up the dormant volcano. During the course of the battle, an unusual event occurred, the marine spotter, who was directing our gunfire, was attacked by Jap soldiers. He was unable to communicate with us by radio for a sustained period of time,

Dangerous Seas

so our captain unwisely decided to assume the spotter's responsibilities. He elevated our 5-inch guns so that the next salvos inadvertently passed over Mt. Suribachi and dropped dangerously close to the battleship *USS Washington*. Instantly over the TBS radio came an excited voice asking, "Who is firing the orange-dyed shells?" Our captain returned the call admitting his mistake and departed at once by whale boat to meet his fate. To this day we never learned the outcome of his meeting with the top brass.

There is a sequel to this story. In the early fifties following the war, Lieutenant Dick Clarke, our gunnery officer, was attending a naval reserve meeting in Boston. The main speaker that day was a retired commodore, former skipper of the *USS Washington*. He told the tale about some crazy destroyer captain who almost sank the *USS Washington* at Iwo Jima. Poor Dick Clarke remained in his seat uncomfortable and unrecognized. To this day the skipper of the USS *Washington* never learned that the gunnery officer of that crazy destroyer was sitting in the audience and listening to his war story.

A few words about our captain, Ronald J. Woodaman. Commander Woodaman came to the *Fraser* with vast destroyer experience, as previously mentioned.

As a human being, he had the respect of the officers and men, but I found him to be hard-hearted, humorless, hot-tempered, and despotic. Moreover, he intimidated some of the officers with his bullying tactics, and he was widely disliked by many of the officers and crew. I clearly recall an incident which resulted in much criticism of Woodaman's judgement. One day, while only a few yards from shore, Woodaman decided to send a dozen or more seamen over the seaward side of the ship to scrape and paint the hull while we were shelling enemy shore installations. With the exception of some sporadic small arms fire, there was little enemy resistance that day. To me this action personified an excessively ambitious man promoting his own advancement by maintaining a shipshape vessel at the expense of the crew. I remember another oddity about Woodaman. During enemy air raids, he occasionally would fire his sidearm, a .45 caliber pistol, at low flying Japanese planes.

On February 23, 1945, D-Day plus 4, we were patrolling about 300 yards off Mt. Suribachi when an historical event occurred. My diary recorded the following: "At 10:35 a.m. the marines raised Old Glory atop Mt. Suribachi after a long struggle. Through binoculars I could see the stars and stripes waiving majestically, a pretty sight to see."

At that moment loud cheers rose from the surrounding ships, as thousands of men saw the American flag blowing over the rocky peak. Instantly, radios crackled with the report of this momentous achievement and flashed the news to the fleet who couldn't see it.

Later that day, a larger flag, measuring eight feet by four feet eight inches, was located on *LST 7799* on the beach below. The new flag was immediately lashed to a long metal pipe. At the summit six marines struggled to drive it into the rubble. Just as the second flag was erected, Joe Rosenthal, an Associated Press photographer, took the most famous picture of World War II.

That night at 8:50 p.m., enemy planes suddenly appeared and attacked our armada that was surrounding the island. The entire fleet, including the *Fraser*, threw up a murderous curtain of antiaircraft fire. It was our first direct participation in shooting at Japanese planes. On that occasion I was at my battle station in the five-inch gun director passing on radar reports of bogies to our gunnery officer, Lieutenant Clarke. Our executive officer, William Ingram, immediately got on the phone from CIC and asked me to evaluate the situation on the outside. I looked out and noticed that our ship was surrounded by numerous large spouts of water rising to some heights. Above the noise of our guns, in my excitement I quickly concluded we were surrounded by bombs hitting the water. Through experience, Ingram promptly and correctly determined that this was only shrapnel hitting the water. So much for my inexperience!

For the next 14 days our naval forces besieging Iwo Jima continued to provide fire support for our marines. Notwithstanding severe casualties, the three marine divisions inched slowly forward. Already two air fields had been captured and were being utilized by our air force. Aboard the *Fraser* we continued to bombard enemy fortifications; at night we illuminated the battlefield with star shells. At times we were at general quarters for more than 24 hours. The continuous firing of our five-inch guns, particularly at night, robbed us of sleep. To compound our problems, our meals deteriorated noticeably; we existed on Spam sandwiches or, more frequently, K rations. In rare moments I learned to catnap, if only for a few minutes. Sleeping for more than three hours became a luxury.

One day, during the shelling of enemy pill boxes and caves, an unusual event occurred. Ashore, a Jap spotter on a radio frequency close to ours then in use, called one of our ships and issued instructions for shore bombardment; "Right a little, up a little." But fortunately the accent was unmistakable, his procedure incorrect, and he was not exactly on the correct frequency.

War had so many horrors that in time one became indifferent to the presence of death. While on patrol off Iwo's shores we frequently encountered the unmistakable odor of bodies rotting on the battlefield, and on occasion we would come upon a corpse floating face down in the water. In death the features of a corpse were often bloated or so badly mangled that positive identification was difficult. The normal procedure was to search the remains for evidence, and then the body was placed in a canvas bag, weighted, and buried at sea. I was reminded of Herman Melville's

Dangerous Seas

words taken from *Billy Budd Foretopman.* "But me they'll lash in hammock drop me deep. Fathoms down, fathoms down, how I'll dream asleep."

The *Fraser* continued her fire support at Iwo Jima until March 7, 1945, when we were replaced by the cruiser *Salt Lake City.* In the company of the *USS Lakewood Victory,* a fleet auxiliary vessel, we had orders to depart for Ulithi in the Caroline Islands. Our course lay directly south into welcomed tropical waters. We reached Ulithi on March 11th and ship's company finally had a chance to catch up on much needed sleep. For us the Iwo Jima Campaign was over.

Meanwhile on March 16th, Major General Harry Schmidt of the Marine Corps announced that Iwo Jima was at last secure. Already the first of many damaged B-29s, returning from raids on Japan, were using the airfields for emergency landings. But the toll was high. Admiral Nimitz announced that all branches of the armed forces, particularly the marines, had suffered 24,127 casualties; 4,189 were killed in action and 19,938 were wounded during the 26 day battle. Approximately 30% of the landing forces were casualties. For the Japanese, 21,000 men were killed. Only 216 wounded prisoners were taken.

On March 14th, a navy chaplain at the battlefield gave this eulogy: "Here lie the officers and men, negroes and whites, rich and poor — together. Here no man prefers another because of his faith or despises him because of color. No prejudices, no hatred. Theirs is the highest and purest democracy."

In the 1960s, some fifteen years after this battle, I had the opportunity to visit the statue commemorating the battle of Iwo Jima in Washington, D.C. It is located on a gentle slope near Arlington National Cemetery. As I stood there alone viewing this life-size replica of the famous flag raising event honoring the marines, I thought about those dark, somber days of long ago, and a marine ditty which said:

And when he gets to heaven
to Saint Peter he will tell,
one more marine reporting,
Sir, I've served my time in hell.

Engraved on the polished marble base of the statue was Admiral Nimitz's famous tribute to the marines at Iwo Jima. "Uncommon Valor Was a Common Virtue."

Dangerous Seas

Okinawa

In my diary I wrote, "Ulithi is a primitive, tropical island where we see natives in aboriginal canoes with colored sails moving about our warships anchored in the harbor. Ashore I observed beautiful white beaches dotted with palm trees. The native huts lining the shore appear to be crudely contstructed of bamboo, have roofs of grass, and are built on poles."

In Ulithi's large harbor rested the famous Task Force 58. Once again warships were gathering for another strike. I saw at least 15 carriers, heavy cruisers, destroyers, minesweepers, ammunition barges, oilers, cargo ships, and various amphibious vessels—*LSD*s, *LST*s, *LCI*s, and *LCT*s.

While remaining at anchor at sunset on March 11th, we watched Jap planes suddenly appear over the harbor and attack the carrier *Randolph*. I was unable to determine the extent of the damage and casualties. As the days passed, more warships continued to gather, particularly mine craft vessels—*DMS*s, *AM*s, and many *YMS*s. During our short stay I was able to talk with other nearby destroyer personnel who recently arrived from the Philippine invasion. Several sailors reported that in desperation almost all Jap pilots have become suicidal. The only defense against the kamikaze was accurate shooting. It was kill or be killed.

On March 18, 1945, we spent the entire day in intense heat taking aboard food, fuel, and ammunition. A large percent of the projectiles were AA common, used principally against aircraft. We were headed for Okinawa, one of 50 islands in the Ryukyu chain between Formosa and Kyushu, Japan. Okinawa is 60 miles long and from 2 to 18 miles wide and largely fringed with reefs. The last American to visit the island was Commodore Perry in May of 1853.

The following day our squadron of destroyer minelayers departed in a convoy consisting of approximately 50-odd minesweepers. At sea the captain announced that our little group had the job of sweeping mine fields off Okinawa's shores prior to landings by our amphibious forces.

Because minesweepers were slow-moving, our convoy traveled at only 8 knots. We were not expected to reach our destination for another 8 days. On our journey north, we encountered very heavy ocean swells which caused all ships to roll and pitch. Because of rough seas, it was difficult to stand and move about. Moreover, the ship's motions made meals a challenge. Any dishes or food on mess tables not secured would slide away. Trying to sleep at night was also a problem due to the ship's constant pitching and rolling. Eventually, on March 23rd, the weather changed for the better.

While underway, one of our lookouts spotted some floating mines passing down our starboard side. We immediately sank them with machine gun fire. Submerged and floating mines were a continuing menace to passing ships. If contact was made with a mine, the explosion was powerful enough to blow a hole in the ship's hull causing her to sink in a matter of minutes. Conversely, floating mines hit by gunfire exploded skyward and were not considered as lethal.

Our little task force of mine craft neared its destination; we were well within Japanese-controlled waters, and I wondered when we would be discovered. All hands were alerted to watch for possible enemy submarines and aircraft, particularly at dawn and at sunset. On March 24, 1945, I recorded in my diary the following, "We are now moving northward at a speed of 12 knots. This evening on the horizon I could see major units of Task Force 58. Evidently they have been shelling Okinawa. It is comforting to know that we are not alone; Japanese aircraft will be our major threat. Tomorrow we reach our destination, the shores of Okinawa. Everyone is naturally on edge. In preparation for battle, we were given photos of tomorrow's targets."

March 25, 1945 was Palm Sunday, and I distinctly remember that it was a beautiful, clear day. Our objective was the occupation of the Kerama Islands, approximately 15 miles southwest of Okinawa. The plan called for the creation of a seaplane base and a fleet anchorage which would support an invasion of Okinawa six days later. At 8:20 a.m. our flotilla of destroyers sailed among these little islands and bombarded the following targets: a railroad, sulphur mine, power plant, and a radio station. In moving along the shoreline in single file, our destroyers at times were within 200 yards from the beach. The surrounding terrain was scenic and mountainous. With field glasses I saw many rice paddies on the hillsides, but no sign of human beings.

During the bombardment our ships used phosphorous shells which were very destructive. On contact, many fires were started, deadly shrapnel was scattered across a wide area, and each projectile emitted poisonous gas. Our warships were certainly easy targets for enemy coastal guns, yet there was no resistance. Perhaps our arrival was a surprise to the enemy.

Meanwhile our sweeps cleared adjoining beaches of mines in preparation for landings by army amphibious forces of the 77th Division. Since we were completely surrounded by active Jap air bases in Saki Shima, China, Formosa, and the Japanese mainland, we expected massive, retaliatory air attacks, but the day ended, strangely enough, without the appearance of enemy action. That first night our 50-odd mine sweepers and our six destroyers quietly sailed into the East China Sea to hide from the prying eyes of enemy planes. This was merely the lull before the storm.

Following the successful seizure of the Kerama Islands, on Easter Sunday, April 1, 1945, the main assault on Okinawa began. The 2nd Marine Division feinted an attack on the east coast while the real invasion occurred on the west coast of the island. The 1st and 6th Marine Divisions, with units

Dangerous Seas

of the 10th Army, landed successfully. At the time we were assigned to a radar picket station south of Okinawa.

In the days that followed, March 26th through April 4th, the *Fraser* was assigned to several radar picket stations off Okinawa. To meet the expected enemy air offensive, the navy established a ring of picket stations, 16 in all, surrounding Okinawa. Each station was manned by destroyers and destroyer-type vessels, to which small gunboats were added to increase fire power. Also, the small gunboats were there to pick up any survivors after an air attack. Our ship affectionately referred to them as "small boys" or "vultures." Our duty at each station was conditioned by our supply of fuel, food, and ammunition. On average, however, we stayed at each station about three or four days. In time radar picket station 1, directly north of the island, was dubbed by our crew as "bogie junction." An assignment to "bogie junction" meant continuous air attacks, no sleep, and casualties. As you would expect, no one wanted duty at "bogie junction."

Picket duty at Okinawa brought about endless enemy air attacks against our ships. A typical air raid might be described as follows: When the familiar and dreaded "Gong, Gong, Gong" sounded over our P.A. system, followed by "ALL HANDS, MAN YOUR BATTLE STATIONS", men instantly tumbled out of their sacks, dropped their books, letters, card games, and coffee cups to proceed to their posts. Instinctively, ship's company, totaling 376 men, moved swiftly and automatically up starboard and down port to battle stations in daylight or total darkness. Within three or four minutes each department reported sequentially to the bridge and CIC. "MOUNT ONE MANNED AND READY.... MOUNT TWO MANNED AND READY.... SONAR MANNED AND READY.... CONTROL MANNED AND READY.... FORWARD ENGINEERING MANNED AND READY...."

At this point the executive officer, Bill Ingram, and the radio technicians gathered in CIC to watch the radar screens as approaching enemy planes were being plotted. The CIC officer, Ensign Phil Clarke, alerted the bridge and the Mark 37 gun director where Dick Clarke, the gunnery officer, two fire controlmen, and I were stationed. Over our phones came the words, "CONTROL, CIC, TARGET BEARING 260. SPEED 250 AND CLOSING RAPIDLY." Lieutenant Dick Clarke responded, "CONTROL, AYE, TRACKING, TRACKING."

Approaching enemy planes were now 22,000 yards away. Our six five-inch guns and 40mms instantly swung around to starboard and pointed skyward towards the onrushing targets. All guns were now locked in with the Mark 37 director. Concurrently, Captain Woodaman called the engine room and gave the order, "ALL ENGINES AHEAD FLANK SPEED." The engine room reacted at once, and *Fraser* lunged ahead to a top speed of about 32 knots. Personnel on the bridge and gunners in their mounts scanned the horizon anxiously for their first glimpse of the onrushing bogies.

Ten thousand yards on the starboard quarter two Jap planes are sighted by the Mark 37 optics and then by lookouts on the bridge. CIC continued its reports to the bridge and control as enemy planes approached.... "RANGE NINE O DOUBLE O....RANGE EIGHT O DOUBLE 0." Over the phones came the captain's order, "COMMENCE FIRING, COMMENCE FIRING." Immediately the three mounts with twin five-inch guns roared into action with the targets now at a distance of 6,000 yards. As the range closed, our 40 and 20mm guns joined in. The noise was earsplitting. Hot, spent shell cases spilled onto the metal decks adding to the din of explosions. A mosaic pattern of smoke puffs surrounded the incoming aircraft.

Miraculously, the two enemy aircraft swiftly passed over our ship mast high and somehow escaped our concentrated barrage. In a matter of seconds the two bogies disappeared into the clouds seemingly undamaged. In retrospect, this entire action took less than three minutes. For the moment, at least, *Fraser* withstood another air attack and survived another day. Our crew was relieved but exhausted.

Dangerous Seas

Kamikazes

On March 29, 1945, while on picket duty off southern Okinawa, the *Fraser* shot down her first enemy plane. It was a clear moonlit night when enemy aircraft appeared over the island in great force. That night over our TBS (Talk Between Ships) came widespread reports of enemy air activity at most of the picket stations. It was the practice of Jap pilots to fly low at night in search of the telltale wakes of ships. Once located, the kamikaze would normally aim for the bridge or fantail, the most vulnerable parts of a ship.

At 1:00 that morning we were called to general quarters, because enemy planes were in the vicinity. Minutes later we returned to our normal watches. I was off duty, so I turned in for some much needed sleep. At 2:50 we were again called to general quarters. Instantly, I jumped from my sack, put on my shoes hurriedly, and raced up the starboard side of the ship headed for the five-inch gun director atop the bridge. Our forward five-inch guns were already firing at three Jap bombers crossing our bow about mast high. At that height they were clearly visible in the moonlight. In my diary I noted, "The *Fearless Fraser* shoots down her first plane, one of three 'Bettys' that crossed our bow low over the water. The moon was bright, visibility clear, and two five-inch salvos made direct hits. The bomber burst into flames and crashed into the sea on our port side." The plane was so close I could clearly see the pilot's head silhouetted against the fiery background of his burning cabin. In a final gesture of defiance, the pilot futilely turned his burning plane towards our ship, but his blazing inferno fell short in a cartwheeling crash into the sea 200 yards from us.

We made a cursory search of the burning wreckage for survivors. There were none. The remains of the bomber continued to burn for about an hour, attracting other Jap planes. Thinking the inferno was a ship, several enemy planes bombed the site. As a result of this action, I wrote, "The morale of the crew is high. After all, it is our first plane."

Meanwhile the kamikazes were taking their toll of ships, particularly destroyers. Already we received reports that the destroyer *Halligan, DD 584*, was sunk by a mine. Also, kamikazes heavily damaged the battleship *Nevada*, BB 36, the light cruiser *Biloxi, CL 80*, and the destroyers *Porterfield (DD 682), O'Brien (DD 725), Callahan (DD 792), Murray (DD 576)*, and the high speed minesweeper *Dorsey (DMS)*.

On March 21, 1945, while we were at battle stations, at 1:00 a.m. a lone Jap plane suddenly appeared low over our mast. It was too close for our five-inch guns, but one of our 40mms hit the aircraft in the belly. Mortally wounded, the pilot circled our convoy for a likely target and attempted to ram a nearby troop transport. He fell short of his objective and crashed into the sea. This was the *Fraser*'s second downed enemy plane.

Three hours later that same morning, 3:48 to be exact, I wrote in my diary, "An unseen enemy aircraft appearing from nowhere swooped in at an altitude of about 200 feet and dropped a bomb that exploded just aft of our fantail. The explosion lifted the stern of the *Fraser* high in the water, and shrapnel raked the after part of the ship. Fortunately there was no damage to personnel or the *Fraser*." At the time of this attack I was off duty and sound asleep in the crew's quarters in the after part of the ship. The noise of the bomb startled me, yet in seconds I found myself racing to my battle station in total darkness. At that time I clearly recall Quartermaster West on the bridge shouting in a frightened, falsetto voice over the P.A. system, "ALL HANDS, MAN YOUR BATTLE STATIONS." I wrote in my diary the following, "We were all scared, because this was our closest call so far. Strange as it may seem, not one gun was trained on this bogie until after he dropped his bomb. Lady luck was again with us. I still can't figure out how the enemy missed us, as it was another moonlit night."

Prior to the amphibious forces landing on Okinawa, we provided antiaircraft protection for our minesweepers off the southern coast, and at night we replaced a ship in our squadron, *Toleman, DM-28*. The night before, the *Toleman* was under attack by at least 10 suicide boats, dubbed "skunks" by the navy. The *Toleman* sank four of the suicide boats; the others fled. These boats traveled at speeds up to 30 knots and carried dynamite, depth charges, or torpedoes. Like the kamikaze planes, these sailors were fanatical and completely disregarded their own safety. It was difficult to understand the oriental mind.

April 1, 1945, was Easter. It was also the day the 10th Army and the First, Second, and Sixth Marine Divisions invaded Okinawa. And at sea there were heavy air raids against the fleet. I wrote in my diary, "It is too bad people at home can't understand or even imagine what a grim life this is. You have to experience this existence to understand fully what men go through. Constant air attacks bring about sensations of fear, anxiety, and utter fatigue compounded by the lack of sleep. Meanwhile more destroyers at picket stations have been damaged, and we wonder when our turn will come. Every night seems to get worse. I am beginning to dread sunsets, knowing that darkness brings about air activity."

On April 2nd, at 3:34 a.m., while under a series of attacks, we gunned down our third enemy aircraft. It was subsequently identified as a "Val", a Jap fighter plane. And that same day at 7:00 a.m., while convoying some transports from the area for the night, our task group came under a violent air raid. From my battle station atop the five-inch guns I watched suicide planes, identified as "Tojos," face the convoy's fire power. During the battle of ships versus planes, one kamikaze crashed a transport, another hit an unidentified destroyer. Two more kamikazes suddenly came out of the clouds and began suicide runs against another transport. The first plane was

Dangerous Seas

shot down by the transport's gunners. The second plane started its suicide run, but as the range rapidly closed, antiaircraft shrapnel tore off a wing causing it to plunge into the sea.

It was a brilliant display of accurate shooting, and our crew cheered at the results. It was almost like a football game where the home team scores a touchdown. We were momentarily joyous over the outcome.

Naval casualties mounted daily, as more warships were damaged by suicide planes. Reports indicated that Jap planes hit the following vessels: destroyer *Adams*, *DM 27*, the cruiser, *Indianapolis*, *CA 35*, cargo vessel, *Wyandot*, *AKA 92*, and the attack transport, *Hinsdale*, *APA 120*.

While the fighting on Okinawa continued, Kerama Retto was secured and quickly turned into a formidable supply and repair base. But the harbor was full of oil, and it became a graveyard of damaged ships, many of them destroyers. I had a chance to go ashore briefly on Kerama Retto to see the sights. In the company of some shipmates, we visited a seaside village to get our first view of Okinawans. Like the Japanese, they were small in stature, on average not over five feet two inches. From all accounts, they led simple, primitive lives, mainly farming rice paddies and fishing. The Japanese treated the Okinawans as inferiors and used them principally for manual labor. Under our occupational forces, Okinawans feared Americans. In time, however, they came to be docile, subservient people. The village itself was rudimentary. The homes were largely two or one room shacks constructed of clay or mud with grass roofs. Farm animals wandered freely on winding dirt roads among the houses. Plumbing facilities were nonexistent. Water was carried to the homes from a central well in the village.

Outside the hamlet was a small cemetery where crypts for the dead were open caves carved in the side of hills. Each family housed the remains of ancestors in jars next to other family heirlooms. During the early days of occupation, many servicemen, particularly sailors, were anxious to acquire Japanese souvenirs, such as rifles, pistols, swords, uniforms, and flags. In their eagerness to obtain these mementos, some personnel actually invaded Okinawan tombs. When the fleeing Jap Army learned of this, they planted mines in some of the internment chambers. Before going ashore that day, our crew was forewarned of this danger.

When I returned to the ship that afternoon, I learned that one sailor returned with a stray dog who eventually became very popular with the crew. She was a friendly mongrel who was appropriately named "Okie." She stayed with us during the entire Okinawan campaign. Her diet was a problem for the cooks, as she would eat only raw fish. Her food supply was partially furnished by one member of the crew who was a dedicated fisherman. Every time we dropped anchor, our fisherman was on the fantail trying his luck with rod and reel.

On April 3rd, I was promoted to sonarman third class. This meant an increase of $12.00 in monthly pay. In the Pacific, there was no place to spend it.

On April 5th, in the middle of the biggest air raids of the campaign, Admiral Sharpe, Commander of Minecraft Pacific, came aboard, and *Fraser*, as temporary flag ship, headed south convoying nineteen transports. Our original destination was Saipan, but the next day *Fraser* and the destroyer *Bache, DD 470*, left the convoy and sailed for Guam at 25 knots. Our trip south from the combat zone was smooth, uneventful, and welcomed. Everyone finally caught up on much needed sleep. We entered the friendly, tropical waters of Guam's harbor on April 8th.

Meanwhile through radio circuits, we learned the fleet was catching hell at Okinawa. On April 6th, more than 275 Jap planes were shot down by our ships and combat air patrols. On that day many of the warships we knew so well were either severely damaged or sunk: the destroyer *Bush, DD 529*, was fatally hit by kamikaze attacks. Other familiar destroyers damaged by suicide planes were *Morris, DD 417, Calhoon, DD 801, Bennett, DD 473, Leutz, DD 481, Newcomb, DD 586, Mullany, DD 528, Harrison, DD 573, Howath, DD 592, Hanesworth, DD 700*, and *Hyman, DD 732*. In addition, two destroyer escorts, *Witter, DE 636*, and *Fieberlina, DE 640* and two high speed minesweepers, *Rodman, DMS 21*, and *Emmons, DMS 21,* sustained heavy losses from Japanese aircraft. Once again the *Thomas E. Fraser* was out of harm's way during the heaviest air attacks of the Okinawan campaign. How long would we be so lucky?

Dangerous Seas

Battleship Yamato

At the time we were in Saipan, the Japanese decided to send remnants of their fleet to Okinawa on a suicide mission. Thus, on April 6th, the day of the biggest Jap air raids, the mighty battleship *Yamato*, the cruiser *Yahaqi*, and eight destroyers left Kyushu for Okinawa to engage the American Fleet. Oddly enough, this task force steamed south through the East China Sea without appropriate air cover. Moreover, the *Yamato* and her escorts had only enough fuel for a one-way trip. After attacking the American surface units, the *Yamato* planned to beach herself. Her big 18-inch guns would then serve as coastal artillery while her crew would join the fighting on land.

The *Yamato* was the newest (built in 1940) and largest battleship of the Imperial Fleet, the pride of the Japanese Navy. Fully loaded, her standard displacement was 69,990 tons. She was 850 feet long with a beam of 121 feet. Her armour plating in thickness ranged from 16 to 19 inches and her fire power was fearsome. She had nine 18-inch guns, twelve 6-inch guns, twelve 5-inch guns, and better than 30 antiaircraft weapons. She carried seven aircraft, had a top speed of 27 knots and had a compliment of 2,500 men. Comparatively speaking, the *Yamato's* tonnage, length, and fire power equaled our Iowa Class of battleships, that is, the *New Jersey*, *Wisconsin*, and *Missouri*.

Once at sea, the *Yamato* was spotted by two American submarines, the *USS Threadfin* and the *USS Hackleback*, who in turn alerted one of several nearby task forces. At 8:23 a.m. on April 7th, 280 planes were launched from the carriers *Belleau Wood*, *Bennington*, *Hornet*, *San Jacinto*, *Bataan*, and *Bunkerhill*. A second wave of 106 planes left the *Intrepid*, *Langley*, and *Yorktown* to join in the attack. By 12:32 p.m. the *Yamato* was mortally wounded from bombs and torpedoes. She went down with all hands at 2:10 p.m. Our carrier planes also sank the cruiser *Yahaqi* and four Jap destroyers. We lost ten aircraft. Japan suffered a major defeat. The battleship era was over, and the Japanese Fleet was no longer a factor in the Pacific war.

Dangerous Seas

Guam, Saipan, and Back to Okinawa

Our brief stay in tropical Guam was a marked change from the temperature at Okinawa. Guam's harbor was sheltered by a long jetty and surrounding high cliffs. For several days we were peacefully moored next to the destroyers *Prichett (DD 561)*, *Wantuck (APD 125)*, *Green (APD 26)*, *Smith (DM 23)*, and *Adams (DM 27)*. Outside of Pearl Harbor, Guam became the largest supply and repair base for our ships in the Pacific.

On April 12th, our surface radar was finally repaired. We took aboard ammunition and stores with plans to depart at once. Somehow I managed to avoid the stores detail by going ashore for the day. Apart from a large recreation area, there wasn't much to see on Guam. I was, however, given the navy quota of two beers, which I gave away. The next day, April 13th, while at morning muster, we were told that President Roosevelt had died suddenly. All of us were shocked at the news.

Five days later our period of rest at Guam came to an end. We sailed northward in the company of the *Gosselin (APD 126)*, and the destroyer *Sproston (DD 576)*. Our destination was Saipan, a nearby island. Once there, I was able to go ashore for more relaxation. I visited the beaches where the marines originally landed. The surrounding palm trees were still shattered and torn from intense gunfire. In addition, I inspected several smashed pill boxes containing captured British coastal guns that were seized by the Japanese at Singapore. In my diary I wrote, "Nearby was a group of submissive Jap prisoners doing manual labor under the watchful eye of marine guards. I am surprised to find how small in stature they are. So, this is the enemy!"

The fighting on Saipan had ended, but the surrounding jungle still harbored a number of starving Jap soldiers who refused to surrender. As a consequence, visitors were warned not to wander from populated areas. A few days before I went ashore, a marine told me about an unexpected nighttime skirmish. During an evening movie for marines, several hungry Japs suddenly emerged from the jungle in search of food. They tried to enter a lighted and guarded food depot, but were instantly shot by alert marine guards. On another occasion, several armed Jap soldiers suddenly appeared from the jungle waving white flags of surrender. As they approached a marine outpost, a Jap officer quickly pulled the pin of a grenade and blew his compatriots to kingdom come. The idea of dying for the emperor was difficult for Americans to comprehend.

After spending four quiet, restful days enjoying Saipan's tropical weather, we weighed anchor on April 20th and set sail for Okinawa once again. Our convoy included the *Gosselin (APD 126)*, *Hadley (DD 774)*, *Sproston (DD 577)*, and a large number of *LST*s. Our course was northwest at a speed of only eleven knots. *LST*s were the slowest craft the navy ever built.

Dangerous Seas

Leisure Moments at Sea

War, in reality, is about death. It is a combination of boredom, fatigue, and sudden terrifying moments. During the times we weren't under fire, life at sea was routine and often monotonous. To overcome boredom, some of us found reading as an escape from reality. Our ship's library, though limited, was a good source of entertainment and humor. For the crew, comic books topped the list of popularity. Magazines such as TIME, LIFE, READER'S DIGEST (although months old) were passed from hand to hand.

We also had a ship's paper printed weekly in our yeoman's office. For something to do, I ran an anonymous column entitled "The Cracker Barrel" in which I poked fun at the crew and chief petty officers. My remarks about officers were more cautious, and comments about the captain were obviously off limits. Because the author of "The Cracker Barrel" remained unknown, I believe my trenchant humor was, by and large, well received. In any event the column kept me busy meeting deadlines.

Aboard ship everyone drank coffee all day long: at meals, on watch, and at battle stations. The sonar shack and CIC were adjoining compartments. Because of this, sonarmen and radar technicians visited back and forth. Since our two compartments housed habitual coffee drinkers, we engaged one of our shipfitters to build a king-size coffee pot to serve the sonarmen and radar technicians. This project was accomplished by truncating the top of an expended five-inch shell. The top of the shell was covered by a brass cover into which we inserted a glass percolation bubble. An electrical coil unit was attached to the bottom of the shell to heat the contents. While our new coffee machine took 30 to 40 minutes to heat, we wound up with at least 30 cups of coffee every day.

Next to our king-size coffee pot was a large supply of sugar and powdered milk. Unexpectedly, our supply of sugar attracted a swarm of cockroaches. On a diet of powdered milk, sugar, and occasional bread taken from the ship's galley, the cockroach population expanded rapidly. The only way we could check their population growth was to scald them with hot coffee or mash them with our coffee mugs. Catching darting cockroaches required some skill. It soon became a daily pastime. If five or more kills were made in a day, the sailor qualified as an ace. Eventually, we kept a written record of our kills on a nearby bulkhead.

Coupled with an addiction to coffee, everyone aboard ship smoked. Cigarettes cost 5¢ a pack, or 50¢ a carton. They were often stale, but we smoked them anyway. My favorite brand was Camels; "Not a cough in a carload." I smoked my first cigarette as soon as I was awake, and continued to smoke in the chow line, during meals, on watch, at general quarters, and during daylight hours. The "smoking lamp" was out while getting underway, dropping anchor, taking on fuel and ammunition, and at night while topside. Like so many others, I soon developed a smoker's cough. But I continued to smoke. In those days we were not warned about the harmful effects of tobacco.

Sick bay aboard the *Fraser* was supervised by Dr. Giles Porter and three pharmacist mates. The pharmacist mates did the routine medical treatments and were called various names by the crew—"Doc," "Shanker Mechanic," and "Pecker Checker." The medical quarters consisted of a small compartment amidships on the port side. Apart from emergencies, sick bay had established hours for outpatient services. Personnel would line up for minor ailments such as colds, sunburn, skin rashes, cuts, bruises, boils, diarrhea, and constipation. Pharmacist mates would then dispense an assortment of pills or salve to cure the ailments. More consequential medical problems like appendicitis, major burns, spinal and head injuries, and emotional problems were reviewed by the doctor who then had the patient transferred to a military hospital (if nearby) or to a major warship with larger and better medical facilities.

During my entire stay aboard the *Fraser* I never once had to visit sick bay. But I did develop a large wart on the palm of my right hand. One day I showed it to Tom Oglby, a radar technician, who had an interest in medicine. After a careful examination, he told me he could cure my wart by treating it with shoe polish. I followed his advice and in time the wart disappeared.

My military duty at sea was confined to an area not exceeding 40 feet in width and 376 feet in length. With a compliment of 376 men, I was forced to get along with my shipmates. Our daily living was what I would describe as "compulsory togetherness." To illustrate, the crew's sleeping quarters were in the after part of the ship. Because of fatigue, I could always sleep, notwithstanding constant interruptions, excessive heat from metal decks and bulkheads, insufficient ventilation, the closeness of canvas sacks, the aroma of men's socks, and the widespread snoring of an exhausted crew. At times these noises generated by rhythmic breathing resembled that of a discordant men's choir.

The ship's head was a shining example of "compulsory togetherness." There were always water restrictions on board, too few showers, too many users. There was always a line to use the sinks, and the coup de grâce was the row of toilets—a long metal trough a foot-and-a-half wide and eight feet long. A fast moving current of sea water passed from one end of the trough to the other. Across the flow of sea water were five toilet seats. At certain times of the day, usually after breakfast, every seat was occupied. Some occupants would bring reading material, some became chatty, others stuck to business, remained silent, appeared embarrassed, and looked neither right nor left.

Dangerous Seas

One day a mischievous crewman decided to create some excitement in the head. Shortly after breakfast, he sat on the seat above the entrance of the incoming sea water and waited until all seats were occupied. Then he took a large wad of toilet paper, rolled it into a ball, set it afire, and dropped it into the rushing current. He watched the burning toilet paper pass under the occupied seats. The results were dramatic. Every seat in the house was vacated in a matter of seconds! From this point forward I always tried to occupy the seat just above the incoming sea water.

Dangerous Seas

Okinawa Again

On May 4, 1945, we received orders to leave Guam for Okinawa again. At dawn we departed alone at 25 knots. On that day my diary read, "Anchors aweigh! The fighting fearless *Fraser* heads back to the land of the begoggled bandy legs—Okinawa, here we come!" Once again, amidst reports of mounting destroyer casualties, the *Fraser* was returning to picket duty. We received word that on average at least two destroyers a night were being badly damaged by kamikazes. Losses were now so common on the picket line that dramatic measures were being proposed to solve the problem. It was suggested that the outer islands might be seized to establish radar stations to save our picket ships. Even submarines were considered as a picket duty alternative.

It often crossed my mind that the *Fraser* had been lucky to date. We had been under severe air attacks and had suffered no casualties. Here in the combat zone, being a survivor was our philosophy. If we survived one kamikaze attack, we made it to the next one. Air attacks at Okinawa were an unending series of violent confrontations. Yet none was important enough to be recorded in history. Ernie Pyle, the famous war correspondent, once said, "No action is minor to the man who loses his life."

I was mindful of a college English course where required reading was Stephen Crane's *The Red Badge of Courage*. The story centered on a young, naive soldier going into battle during the Civil War for the first time. The youthful recruit expressed thoughts of hope, fear, and his own mortality. In effect, a death in war was commonplace, cruel, and totally indifferent to human life. I, too, experienced these emotions. In time we all developed what is now called traumatic stress syndrome.

On May 7, 1945, we reached Okinawa, refueled at sea, and were assigned to a picket station southwest of the island. The next day, May 8th, we received good news. I wrote in my diary, "Official word has just been received. Germany has surrendered. The European war is over. Thank God for the wonderful news!"

This time on picket duty we witnessed some morale boosters: the army had introduced new night fighters called "Black Widows." They were assigned to some of our picket stations and we were grateful. Also, the navy increased our air cover at night with our own "night chicks." Now a greater number of kamikazes were being shot down long before they reached our picket stations.

On May 12th, we entered Hagushi Harbor on the west coast of Okinawa and awaited further orders. Units of the Fifth Fleet were also anchored there after shelling the southern coast of the island. In the distance we could hear the rumble of artillery from the 10th Army bombarding enemy installations.

Okinawa, except for the southern tip, was now under our control. While anchored, we listened to radio conversations of our pilots during air attacks. We heard the familiar "Bandits at eight o'clock," "Tally Ho," and "I got him." Then we watched for the trail of smoke in the sky as the doomed Jap plane plunged into the sea. We owed so much to our marine and navy pilots.

At 6:30 p.m. that night I was on the ship's fantail washing clothes in a bucket of soapy water when general quarters was suddenly sounded. Before I could run to my battle station, I looked up and saw two Jap planes coming in low over the harbor. At that moment practically every ship in the anchorage commenced firing. In my diary I wrote, "The first plane started a suicide dive on the battleship *New Mexico* about two hundred yards from us. It was immediately shot down by accurate antiaircraft fire. The second plane began its downward dive with its machine guns firing. It crashed into the superstructure of the *New Mexico* causing enormous explosions and gasoline fires."

We offered our assistance, but the *New Mexico* declined. A harbor tug quickly appeared to extinguish the fires and attend to the wounded. As usual, our captain claimed the *Fraser*'s guns brought down the two Jap planes. I questioned this claim, because every warship in the harbor was firing.

Later that evening, just before dark, some army personnel came alongside in a small boat. They saw one of our cooks dumping canned hot dogs overboard. The soldiers immediately retrieved the discarded food and pleaded for any remaining hot dogs. Our cooks willingly obliged. Our army friends departed triumphantly with their spoils. After that episode I realized that the navy routinely gave three squares a day. The army didn't.

From May 13th to the 23rd the *Fraser* was continuously at sea on various picket stations around Okinawa. Our sea patrols were interrupted only when we returned to Hagushi Harbor to take on a supply of ammunition, fuel, and food. During this duty we put up with at least three or four air raids every day. If we were anchored in Hagushi Harbor during a raid, the alternative to antiaircraft fire was the use of smoke screens to protect our ships. But smoke screens caused eye irritations and breathing difficulties. And sitting quietly under a blanket of smoke did have its anxious moments. There were many nights in the harbor when our ships would wait in suspense as enemy planes appeared and passed over us mast high in search of warships to bomb or crash.

On May 29, 1945, we were ordered to picket duty off Ie Shima, a small island three-and-a-half miles from the northern tip of Okinawa. On Ie Shima were several recently captured air fields which were being repaired so our planes would have another base from which to attack the Japanese homeland. Ie Shima was also the island where Ernie Pyle, the well known and beloved war correspondent, died at the hands of an enemy sniper.

Our patrol consisted of the *Fraser*, a destroyer escort, and several *LCIs*.

Dangerous Seas

At this location we had two Navy F4U Corsairs circling above us during the daytime. But at dusk our air cover returned to their carrier. In the evening we were alone. Starting at 6:30 p.m. that night we were put on general quarters for eleven straight hours, during which time we experienced the heaviest raids of the war. That evening approximately 165 Jap planes in waves came down from the north. They flew directly over our station to attack the air fields on Ie Shima. Ensign Phil Clarke in CIC would normally report to the five-inch gun director the number and location of all "bogies" on his oscilloscope. That night I remember him saying, "There are so many 'bogies' on my screen, I don't know what to tell you." Meanwhile, formation after formation of enemy planes passed over us. Fortunately they ignored our antiaircraft fire. Their objective was to bomb Ie Shima's air fields.

In my diary I wrote that "To reach their objective, Jap bombers had to cross directly over us. They flew in low and dropped their bombs squarely on the designated targets. A line of explosions followed, one after another, momentarily illuminating the skies. During that long night many enemy planes were shot down by night fighters, marine antiaircraft, and our little group of picket ships. The *Fraser* was credited with at least two enemy planes." Later that same evening, our fire-control system broke down. Henceforth, the firing of our guns had to be done manually. I never felt so helpless.

In the early dawn a Jap "Libby" bomber actually landed on an airstrip and deplaned 23 suicide personnel. Before they were killed, they succeeded in destroying several army planes and some supply depots. From our ship I could plainly see a number of fires and explosions on the island silhouetted against the first tinge of the morning sunrise.

This was the longest night of the war for me. Although our picket station was not attacked during these raids, the thought of all those planes crossing our path made me fearful that we would eventually be hit. I clearly remember my reactions that night. I perspired heavily, had a rapid pulse, and my tongue swelled so that I had difficulty talking on the phone with CIC. And my fears were doubled when our fire-control system broke down. I wrote in my diary, "The arrival of sunrise brought a temporary end to the air attacks, and we were grateful. Once again the *Fraser* survived another day unharmed."

When there were quiet moments at sea I used to read the Bible for answers to this crazy world I found myself in. Here carnage on the open seas was a daily occurrence. In the solitude of a clear night I often wondered about man's brief tenure on earth as compared to the ageless stars above and the universe beyond. I pondered the irresolute and eternal questions that have confronted mankind from the beginning of time. How did the universe evolve? Why was it created? Why were we given birth? What is our destination? For one who sought the source of his being, there were no ready answers.

Dangerous Seas

Torpedo Attack

On June 1, 1945, the *Fraser* was directed to patrol the waters off the Jap-held island of Kume, some 20 miles west of southern Okinawa. Intelligence reports indicated that Kume had an active radio station and usable airfield. Our little flotilla of ships was composed of the destroyers *Smith*, *Cassin Young*, and *Fraser*. In addition, we were accompanied by five amphibious craft we called "lobsters."

At 6:00 p.m. that evening at sunset our formation was patrolling in single file. As usual, we were at general quarters at the close of a clear, sunny day. By chance I was idly scanning the horizon through the optics in the five-inch gun director. About four miles out I noticed two unidentified planes flying just above the water on a parallel course with our formation. After closer examination I also noticed that each plane was carrying what appeared to be a torpedo. From our training we were aware that American torpedo planes carried their torpedoes in the plane's belly, unless the bombay doors were opened for a torpedo run.

Apparently these were enemy planes, so I called CIC to check their "IFF" (information friendly or foe). They were immediately identified as Jap planes. We continued to track the two "bogies," and seconds later they turned and headed directly towards our formation for a torpedo run. The first plane, flying only a few feet above the water, attacked the *Smith*, the lead ship in our formation. The torpedo missed its mark. The second plane, also only a few feet over the water, swiftly approached the *Fraser*. Meanwhile, antiaircraft from our ships filled the sky with a mosaic pattern of black bursts of smoke that surrounded the incoming plane. The intruder continued his collision course, undaunted by the unbelievable concentration of gunfire. The noise of our guns plus the spilling of spent shells hitting our metal decks was deafening. When the Jap plane was within 500 yards of our ship, he dropped his "fish" and roared mast high over us. He was so close I could see the bright red circles on the plane's wings. At that very moment the captain shouted out the command, "Hard right rudder" and the *Fraser*, now at flank speed, heeled heavily to starboard. She turned into the oncoming torpedo just in time to see it pass harmlessly down our port side.

From my station above the bridge, I watched the enemy plane rapidly disappear over the horizon, apparently unharmed. After this encounter we knew the two attackers were "Kales," Japanese torpedo planes. In retrospect, Captain Woodaman's cool leadership under fire saved our ship. Once again, it was a close call.

Dangerous Seas

Typhoon

On June 4th, all ships in the area were alerted to a typhoon approaching the Ryukyus Islands. This was the beginning of the typhoon season in the East China seas. A large, threatening storm was moving towards Okinawa from the south. At dawn the next day, the *Fraser* left Kerama Retto in a small convoy headed for Hagushi Harbor on the west coast of Okinawa. At sea our barometer dropped rapidly, and fast-moving, ominous clouds suddenly blanketed the sky. The winds grew in intensity, sporadic sheets of rain began to beat horizontally against the ship, and our vision at sea became partially obscured by the violence of the storm.

It soon became difficult to determine where the sea stopped and the sky began. All ship's compartments were dogged tight. The growing turbulence of the weather became more and more threatening. Topside working parties lashed themselves to lines to avoid being thrown into the violent sea. They risked their lives to secure sliding equipment from crashing into bulkheads. The angry ocean, accompanied by the increasing roar and moaning of violent winds, began to convulse. Our little ship labored helplessly as she rolled and pitched in the towering and agitated white-capped waves.

At times our bow and bridge were submerged by tons of foaming, angry water. And as the winds howled, the *Fraser* fell into enormous troughs and was slow to answer the helm. As we rocked and tossed about like little chips, the ship's company felt the full fury of the storm. The inclinometer on the bridge at times registered 30 degrees. It became a struggle to survive.

Somehow our battered convoy finally reached the relative safety in Hagushi Harbor where we dropped anchor. The storm continued on into the night. Even though we were anchored, our engines continued at 15 knots to prevent our ship from drifting into other vessels. At midnight, the roaring winds slowly abated. The storm was over. In the early light of dawn, the *Fraser* had drifted halfway across Hagushi Harbor, but she was safe. All about us were damaged vessels, including several transports and cargo ships beached by the fury of the gale. In the aftermath of this great typhoon we were a thankful but spent crew forever mindful of the awful violence of a lawless sea.

When it was over, I thought about my boyhood days in church at Deerfield Academy where we sang one of my favorite hymns:

> *Eternal Father, strong to save,*
> *Whose arm doth bind the restless wave,*
> *Who bidd'st the mighty ocean deep*
> *Its own appointed limits keep,*
> *O, hear us when we cry to thee*
> *For those in peril on the sea!*

During the remaining days of June 1945, ship's company experienced many changes for the good. We continued to have daily air raids by Jap planes, but our naval air patrol was noticeably strengthened. Fewer enemy aircraft were breaking through the screen and reaching our ships. Those planes that did reach the fleet were "splashed" with less effort. In conversations with our pilots, we learned that the Japs, due to heavy losses in flight personnel and aircraft, had few reserves left. We learned of bizarre incidents where downed enemy planes were piloted at times by women and even boys. One day, to everyone's surprise, an enemy plane appeared with American markings, but it was unsuccessful in breaking through our defenses. It was promptly shot down by our Corsairs.

In reviewing my diary, I noted that from March 26th, the day we invaded Kerama Retto, through the month of June, the *Fraser*'s crew went to general quarters 175 times because of air raids. This total did not include our daily dawn and sunset calls to battle stations. Over 94 days, this was an average of almost two raids per day. In retrospect, over the same period of time we experienced long hours of labor, daily tension, very little sleep, and endless fatigue.

When not on watch, at battle stations, or work detail, our exhaustion was so complete that I could fall asleep anywhere at any time in unlikely places. I could sleep soundly in a chair with my head against a bulkhead, or prone on a metal deck with my life preserver as a pillow. Boatswains were forever rousing dozing sailors to chip and paint the ship's decks, a necessary but unending process in battling rust. Now that I was a petty officer, I was able to avoid this thankless job.

Leisure moments at sea always involved poker and crap games for high stakes. The usual bull sessions and sailors' barnyard talk involved girls, shore leave, sea duty on different ships, and events at home. One career sailor named Stanley Rumbaugh repeatedly gave his dissertation on what was wrong with the navy and how he would fix it. Ironically, he joined the navy before Pearl Harbor and planned to make the service his career.

The greatest morale builder was mail call, an occasion when we had letters from home. Mail call was a happy event when we had news from parents, wives, girls, and friends. It was also a time when we received photos of girls, wives, newborns, care packages of food, and notices of sickness and death. As we watched and listened to various stories from home, we shared in each other's joys and sorrows

Dangerous Seas

Thoughts of Home

I can still picture my mother's firm handwriting on the weekly letters she wrote. My father, on the other hand, typed his messages on an old, battered Olivetti typewriter. His comments, though brief, were rich in wisdom, philosophy, and self-deprecating humor. My father graduated Phi Beta Kappa from Yale and spent his entire career there as an English professor, educator, writer, and scholar in American Literature.

I didn't apply to Yale. While my father never said anything, to this day I have often wondered if this was a great disappointment to him. Frank Boyden, the headmaster at Deerfield Academy, frequently selected the appropriate college for his seniors. In 1941, a large number of our graduating class, due to his influence, applied to Amherst, Williams, and Wesleyan. In my case, he recommended Wesleyan. I applied nowhere else. In retrospect, had I applied to Yale, my marginal grades might have resulted in a rejection.

Speaking of mail, the *Fraser* was constantly on the move. Weeks would pass before we received any letters from home. Similarly my parents had no mail from me for months at a time, so with some concern, my mother approached a close friend whose father was a retired admiral. He put her at ease by reporting that the *Thomas E. Fraser* was safe and sound somewhere in the wide Pacific.

During wartime all mail going to the States was subject to strict censorship. During the Iwo Campaign, I was able to identify our location, and, at the same time, circumvent the censors. My parents would categorically number my letters by postmark, and I addressed the envelopes "Mr. and Mrs. Stanley T. Williams." While at Iwo, however, I replaced my father's middle initial in successive letters with "I," then "W," and finally "O." They immediately understood my code and knew my whereabouts.

During moments of relaxation at sea, I often thought of my carefree boyhood days on Cape Cod. In 1922, my family purchased a quaint Cape Cod cottage, including a barn and eight acres of land on a hill overlooking Bass River in South Yarmouth. It was the second oldest house in the town. It was built before the American Revolution and at various times served as a Quaker Meeting House.

At the close of Yale's spring semester each year, my parents made plans to return to Cape Cod until fall. In the 1930s, we normally had the use of one car, except for the annual trips to the Cape. Every spring it was my father's custom to purchase a large, secondhand car big enough to transport his books, children's bicycles, pets, family, and innumerable suitcases. Over the years the purchase price of these seasonal vehicles, at best, never exceeded $100. During the 1930s, we drove used Model Ts, Reos, Studebakers, and Packards. Dad's greatest pride and joy was the year he acquired a vintage green 1934 Pierce-Arrow touring car.

It was an impressive vehicle with a patched canvas top and cracked, yellow isinglass curtains. The headlights were built into the front fenders. On the spacious running boards were expandable, metal luggage racks. Also, on the left running board rested a small tool chest for road emergencies. On the rear of the automobile was a spare tire. Inside were two luxurious, black leather seats which could easily accommodate six passengers, not counting two jump seats that folded into the back of the front seat.

Our trips to the Cape, a distance of some 180 miles, normally took the better part of a day, or possibly two days if we encountered road trouble. One hazardous spot along the way was a steep hill in Easthampton, Connecticut. I recall the time when our Model T was so loaded down with passengers and baggage, we couldn't climb Easthampton hill. Dad finally reached the top by putting the Model T in reverse and he backed up the hill.

On another occasion, I remember a Cape trip when my brother and I were in the rumble seat of an old Ford. We were slowly descending a steep hill when a detached auto wheel passed us on the highway. To our surprise, it was the left rear wheel of our Ford. In spite of only three wheels, our car remained level and continued to the bottom of the hill. We reattached the wheel and continued on our journey.

Dad's summer schedule was interesting. He kept a small office in our pump house where he wrote and did research on notable American authors: Herman Melville, Nathaniel Hawthorne, Emerson, Whittier, Longfellow, and Mark Twain. Because his morning schedule was frequently interrupted by visitors and children, he avoided these intrusions by driving his Pierce-Arrow to Flax Pond, a small isolated lake nearby, which could only be reached by an unmarked dirt road. To seek complete seclusion, he drove his car off the dirt road into the surrounding brush like a Sherman tank in search of an appropriate location. Once satisfied, he put down the top and sat in a folding beach chair in the back seat of his Pierce-Arrow. There among his books and papers he was able to study and write undisturbed.

When dad was using the pump house or barn for his office, his constant companion was his pipe. But it never stayed lit. As a consequence, discarded paper and wooden matches often littered his desk and the floor. In an effort to placate mother's strong disapproval of his indifference to orderliness, he bought an empty ten-gallon milk can from a local farmer. Henceforth, this receptacle would be the repository for discarded matches. As the milk can began to fill, his collection of used matches created some notoriety. Neighbors and friends would stop by to view the progress, so he put a large sign on the milk can noting the date his collection started. I think it took him about five years to fill that milk can.

Out in the Pacific, I often thought about my pre-war days with the

Dangerous Seas

family: fishing trips to Nickerson Park in Brewster; our picnics on Nauset Beach, blue berrying, crabbing, clamming, and sailing our boat on Bass River. Those were the halcyon days of my youth. (Today, in remembrance of my father, I carry in my wallet a quotation from Mark Twain. It reads, "When I was a boy of fourteen, my father was so ignorant I could hardly stand to have him around. But when I got to twenty-one, I was astonished at how much he had learned in seven years.")

Dangerous Seas

Victory at Okinawa

On June 25, 1945, we received a welcomed announcement: the ground war at Okinawa was coming to an end. With the exception of a few small, isolated pockets, Okinawa was now under our control. For the first time in the war, Japanese soldiers surrendered in great numbers. They finally recognized the futility of a continued struggle. But enemy air attacks persisted against our ships around Okinawa. However, Jap aircraft became less effective primarily due to our vastly improved air defenses, inexperienced enemy pilots, and the expansion of B-29 bombings of Japan. From all reports we received, our B-29s rained total havoc on the enemy.

Each day I watched large B-29 formations flying north and then south at very high altitudes. One day, while under attack by suicide planes, a low flying B-29 suddenly emerged from the clouds and our trigger-happy gunners opened fire. The B-29 was immediately identified as friendly aircraft, so the captain quickly ordered "cease firing" over the P.A. Fortunately, no harm was done. But I am sure the pilots and crew were visibly shaken by our inadvertent actions. This wasn't the first or last time jittery gunners unintentionally fired on friendly ships or planes.

The *Fraser* spent the balance of June in Kerama Retto. One night while at anchor in the harbor, Jap planes suddenly appeared and orders were given not to fire. This time our improved night fighter patrols took over. All ships became an audience to a great display of air tactics. The most spectacular incident of the evening occurred when a Jap bomber, a "Betty," was hit high over our ship. The ill-fated bomber caught fire and exploded into a thousand pieces and illuminated the sky like fireworks. Undoubtedly this aircraft was loaded with tons of explosives. Again, accolades went to our marine and navy pilots who were now giving us excellent protection.

During the final days of June, the *Fraser* was engaged in several mine sweeping missions in the Yellow Sea about 100 miles west of Okinawa. Our task force usually consisted of five or more destroyer mine layers and sixty-odd *YMS*s (Yard Mine Sweepers), under the safeguard of two circling Navy Corsairs.

Mine sweeping was always a dreary business. It was not only tiring and dangerous, but at times deadly. Our *YMS*s were wooden vessels ranging from 60 to 80 feet long. They were lightly armed having only a 3-inch antiaircraft gun and two 20mm machine guns. *YMS*s had a compliment of about 20 officers and men. Somehow, intelligence always knew the whereabouts of Jap mine fields. And when located, our mine sweepers would fan out and proceed slowly in formation over the mine field, towing long, submerged wire cables. Attached to the end of these cables were metal cutters called paravanes. On contact with a mine, the paravane would sever the cable and the mine would rise rapidly to the surface. It was then destroyed by small arms fire from the destroyers following the *YMS* formation.

Once the mine fields were cleared, the *Fraser* and other destroyers in the flotilla would drop buoys marking the swept areas. Submerged mines were always a deadly menace to passing warships, but once on the surface hits by small arms fire would cause explosions harmlessly skyward. Enemy mine fields were of two types—controlled or independent. For example, mines laid in harbor defense installations (the Panama Canal) were electronically controlled. Each mine was wired to a system enabling the base ashore to determine whether the mines blocking the passageway were to be activated or not. By and large, the Japanese Navy used independently-moored mines in the open seas around Japan.

Sweeping mines was also a slow process, going no faster than eight knots for an average duration at sea from four to ten days. Our task force would normally start sweeping at sunrise until about four o'clock in the afternoon. Our missions took us near the coasts of Formosa, China, Korea, and eventually Japan. Because our *YMS*s were lightly armed, lacked speed, and because of our proximity to enemy territory, I was always fearful of enemy air raids. On more than one occasion we were observed by reconnaissance planes, but I can't recall any time when our sweeping operations away from Okinawa were interrupted by enemy air attacks.

During sweeping missions, and depending on the number of mines that were brought to the surface, we listened to continuous explosions as our gunners, using Browning automatic rifles, poured small arms fire into the floating mines. One late afternoon I was off watch having a cigarette on deck just outside the sound shack. By chance, I spotted a partially submerged horned mine slide harmlessly by in the wash of our slip. I alerted the bridge, and the captain reversed course to find it, but without success. This was another close call for the *Fraser*. Over a period of time, some mines became waterlogged and did not explode when hit by gunfire, yet they continued to be a constant navigational hazard to our ships.

Dangerous Seas

Atomic Bomb

In July of 1945, it became increasingly clear that Japan was close to defeat. Four years earlier their surface fleet was the third largest in the world and dominated the Pacific. Now, because of U.S. action and a shortage of fuel, the Japanese surface fleet was no longer a threat to the growing might of our naval forces. Our Third Fleet was presently sailing off the coast of Japan. We were bombing and shelling their coastline at will.

In the interim, the *Fraser* was expanding her sweeping missions to Formosa, Korea, and the coast of China. On the 16th of July we returned to Okinawa because of a leak in a forward compartment. Before entering a floating dry dock, all of our ammunition had to be removed. This task took the crew a full day. Once in dry dock, all hands went over the sides to scrape and paint the hull while the leak was repaired. After leaving dry dock, we hurriedly returned the ammunition to the magazines and sailed 300 miles south of Okinawa to avoid another approaching typhoon.

On July 20th we returned to Okinawa once more and the captain advised ship's company that our sweeping missions in the East China Sea had been successfully completed. He added that we would probably head for Leyte in the Philippines for a well-deserved rest. The next day, July 21st, it was announced that our skipper, Commander Ronald J. Woodaman, was being reassigned. On his day of departure, we mustered briefly for the captain's comments. After bidding farewell to ship's company, Woodaman saluted the colors, the officer of the deck, and crossed the gangway for the last time amidst muffled boos from the crew. There was no sorrow in his departure. Commander Woodaman was not a popular captain.

One final comment about Commander Woodaman. When the *Fraser* and other warships were fighting off swarms of enemy planes, and one or more were "splashed" by ships' gunners, very often it was impossible to know which ship or ships scored the fatal hits. Nevertheless, Woodaman almost always sought credit for the kills, even though many of his claims, in my judgement, were questionable. According to custom, the *Fraser* painted seven Jap flags on her bridge. When entering port or lining up alongside another warship, it was common practice to count a ship's Jap flags. The bridges of some warships were covered with many enemy flags, so one would logically conclude that here was a "fighting ship." I somehow felt that Woodaman was too ambitious and too self-serving. I believe he promoted the *Fraser*'s accomplishments for his own advancement. Our new captain was Commander Nevitt B. Atkins, a fine officer and gentleman, greatly admired by the officers and crew.

In retrospect, statistics now indicated that between April 6 and June 22, 1945, the end of the Okinawan Campaign, there were ten large organized kamikaze attacks employing a total of 1,465 planes, as shown in the following statistics:

Date of Attack	Total	Navy Planes	Army Planes
6-7 April...	355	230	125
12-13 April...	185	125	60
15-16 April...	165	120	45
27-28 April...	115	65	50
3-4 May...	125	75	50
10-11 May...	150	70	80
24-25 May...	165	65	100
27-28 May...	110	60	50
3-7 June...	50	20	30
21-22 June...	45	30	15
Totals......	1,465	860	605

28 warships were sunk and 225 were damaged by Japanese air action. Destroyers sustained more hits than any other class of ships.

On July 22, 1945, while resting at anchor in Buckner Bay, Okinawa, I wrote in my diary, "Sensational rumor, Japan wants peace and is offering us all territory except Japanese homeland. The end is approaching!"

On July 29th, the destroyer *Callaghan (DD 792)* was sunk off radar picket station # 9. Ironically, on July 27th, two days before, their captain announced to a jubilant crew that the *Callaghan* had orders in a few days to return to San Francisco for repairs and a well-deserved rest. On that fateful night of July 29th, a single kamikaze approached, turned off his engine, and glided silently into the *Callaghan*'s after deck house. The explosions that followed set off a series of fires, and in minutes the *Callaghan* was dead in the water. About an hour later she sank. Out of a compliment of about 370 men, one officer and 46 men went down with the ship. Of her survivors, two officers and 71 of the crew suffered wounds from the attack. The *Fraser* operated with *Callaghan* on several missions. She was the last American destroyer to be lost in World War II.

On August 7, 1945, the *Fraser* was moored in Buckner Bay when we received the following dramatic report, as recorded in my diary, "Sensational news has just been released. A B-29 bomber just dropped an atomic bomb on Hiroshima, Japan. Supposedly this new bomb is the most devastating weapon ever developed by science. Does this mean we won't have to invade Japan? If this new missile is as powerful and destructive as reports say, it brings an entirely new outlook on the war."

Without exception, our ship was ecstatic over this good news. But with

Dangerous Seas

good news came bad news. We also received a radio report that the cruiser *Indianapolis* (*CA 35*) was torpedoed off Guam with a great loss of life. The *Fraser* performed shore bombardment at Iwo Jima with the *Indianapolis*. (After the war it was revealed that the *Indianapolis* delivered the first atomic bomb to Tinian Island. Was her fate at the hands of a Japanese submarine poetic justice?)

The end of the war was now in sight. The Soviet Union declared war on Japan on August 9th, and at the same time a second atomic bomb was dropped on the city of Nagasaki. Japan was given an ultimatum to "surrender or die." The following day, August 10th, radio reports stated that Japan was suing for peace, but they asked to keep their emperor. Everyone was jubilant over the wonderful news.

On Okinawa, military personnel prematurely began firing thousands of rounds of ammunition into the sky to celebrate. During the night the sky was illuminated by small arms fire. The occasion resembled a fourth of July celebration.

But the war continued for us. At 9: 00 p.m. on August 10th, we went to battle stations because of a low-flying enemy plane. Unexpectedly it flew into Buckner Bay and dropped a torpedo or bomb on one of the old ladies of the fleet, the battleship *Pennsylvania*. There was no immediate report of casualties. At dawn on August 13th, the *Fraser*, as part of a task force, weighed anchor. We left Okinawa headed north, 050 degrees at 22 knots. Our destination was Japan. Rumors persisted that we would rendezvous with Admiral Halsey's Third Fleet somewhere off the Japanese coast. We were told that our mine sweeping units would sweep Tokyo Bay before our warships could enter. If true, this would be an historic undertaking.

Dangerous Seas

Peace

On August 15, 1945, we became part of an enormous task group composed of six or seven carriers, twelve cruisers, twenty-two destroyers, plus fleet tankers and other auxiliary vessels. In addition, several British destroyers and the British battleship *Duke of York* joined our armada. While waiting for the Japanese to surrender, overhead we saw B-29 formations continuing their bombing runs over Japan. Later, the same day, we received the most wonderful news in a flash that came over our wires. It said, "The United States confirms the report that Japan has surrendered unconditionally!" The officers and crew of the *Fraser* were ecstatic. (The killing time had ended.)

During the ensuing days, more warships gathered in a show of strength not far from Tokyo Bay. We were waiting for orders to land occupation forces. I recall standing on the bridge and commenting to others that we were surrounded by hundreds of warships. For a short time we sailed alongside the battleship *Missouri*. To the sailors, she was affectionately known as the "Mighty Mo." I put my field glasses on the *Missouri* and, by chance, saw Admiral "Bull" Halsey pacing the bridge. At the time Halsey created quite a stir when he stated publicly that he intended to ride the emperor's white horse.

On the 17th of August, the *Fraser* and the destroyer *Gwin* (*DM 33*) were suddenly ordered to Iwo Jima to pick up mail for Task Force 38. When our two ships reached Iwo the next day, we were ceremoniously greeted by two low-flying P-51 Mustangs who asked permission to buzz our ships for practice. They moved in and out so fast our gunners couldn't track them. Many changes took place since our ship was last at Iwo. Military engineers had truncated Mt. Suribachi with explosives. To the north the reconditioned airfields were substantially enlarged and crowded with aircraft and equipment. This bleak, stone fortress was converted into several giant airfields crammed with B-29s, B-17s, P-51s, P-47s, A-26s, B-26s, C-47s, and A-28s. In my diary I noted, "Air power certainly played a major role in hastening the defeat of the Japanese. Even though the marines paid a heavy price to seize this unattractive, desolate, rocky piece of real estate, their valiant efforts saved the lives of thousands of pilots and crews." We immediately picked up 350 bags of mail and some British officers, and sailed north to rejoin Task Force 38.

At sea on August 19th, a submarine unexpectedly surfaced off our port bow. Orders were promptly given to train all guns on the target until she was identified. She turned out to be the American submarine *Trutta* (*421*) in a sanctuary zone, headed for The United States. Late that same day we spotted Task Force 38 on the horizon. It was by far the biggest armada of ships that I have ever seen. The *Fraser* refueled from the battleship *Iowa*

(BB 61) and then spent the next two days delivering mail to approximately 20 warships.

We were told that our delay in sailing to Tokyo Bay was caused by the late arrival of occupation forces. Apparently marine units en route from the Philippines ran into some severe storms deferring the date of occupation. At the time a rumor circulated among some of the ships. Without the availability of marine and army landing forces, as an interim, I was told the navy was considering landing several thousand armed blue jackets. Moreover, this occupation force would be comprised of mostly single men. Even though I never learned to handle a rifle in the navy, I pictured myself going ashore out-numbered by a savage enemy bent on unlimited guerrilla warfare. Fortunately, this was only a rumor. Besides, our marines eventually arrived for occupation duty. Bless their souls!

Finally, at dawn on August 25, 1945, our task force changed course and headed directly for Tokyo Bay about 150 miles away. Two days later there was great excitement aboard ship. At 11:27 a.m. we sighted the snow-capped, famous Mt. Fujiyama. These magnificent mountains, rising majestically in the clouds, were truly an imposing sight to observe from the sea. As darkness fell, the *Fraser* and other mine craft vessels dropped anchor in Sagami Wan, a quiet port dominated by a towering but distant Mt. Fujiyama. Our anchorage for the night was only a few miles southwest of Tokyo Bay. This was our first night in Japan.

Dangerous Seas

Tokyo Bay

At dawn on August 28, 1945, the *Fraser* with her "sweeps" approached the entrance to Tokyo Bay and began to clear the area of possible mines. At 11:00 a.m. we went to battle stations, and our flotilla of 24 ships proudly entered Tokyo Bay in single file at a speed of 14 knots. For our protection, hundreds of Navy Wildcats and Corsairs filled the sky above us. This occasion was a tense, dramatic and gratifying moment in our young lives.

To celebrate, Captain Atkins ordered a new American flag be hoisted to the yardarm to mark our hard-fought victory. The first American ships to enter Tokyo Bay were as follows:

10 Yard Mine Sweepers
4 Auxiliary Mine Sweepers
Ellyson (DMS 19)
Hambleton (DMS 20)
Fraser (DM 24)
Southernland (DD 746)
Twining (DD 540)
San Diego (CL 53)
Gosselin (APD 26)
Wedderburn (DD 684)
Cumberland Sound (AV 17)
Suisin (AVP 53)

The entrance to Tokyo Bay was about three to four miles wide. However, once inside, the Bay expanded considerably. At my battle station I clearly remember scanning the shoreline on both sides for any signs of human life or activity. There were none. I wondered if the immediate area had been purposely evacuated.

Farther inside the Bay, our formation came upon widespread destruction. About us rested remnants of the once proud Imperial Japanese Navy brought to her knees by our air power. I saw Japanese warships of every description either abandoned, sunk, or beached. Of particular interest was a large, deserted battleship of the *Nagato* class lying on her side. Her beams were torn open by explosions, her superstructure shattered, but her guns were still pointing skyward as if in a final act of defiance.

Our mission was to seize and occupy the Yokosuka Naval Base. Marines were already ashore and had the "situation well in hand." Farther inland on the horizon I could see the big steel city of Yokohama. It was totally destroyed by air attacks. Our little flotilla of warships finally dropped anchor at 1: 47 p.m. at the Yokosuka Naval Base. Within minutes a comical-looking, battered Jap tug approached our ship as a peace emissary. Aboard were little puppet-like, uniformed military personnel who appeared nervous and anxious to please us. At our commands, they smiled, bowed frequently and were totally subservient. Apparently the emperor had told his subjects not to resist. We subsequently learned that the Japanese obeyed this royal edict without exception.

At sunrise the next day, we led 14 minesweepers to a mine field outside Tokyo Bay where we successfully surfaced a large number of moored mines. At 1:00 p.m. we returned to Yokosuka Naval Base convoying some British warships, *The Duke of York*, *King George V*, and the hospital ship, *Marigold*. At the same time several troop transports arrived and discharged additional marines. They immediately went ashore to assist in occupation duties. By late afternoon Tokyo Bay was crowded with heavy cruisers, destroyers, tankers, destroyer tenders, cargo vessels, repair ships, and an assortment of amphibious craft. I also watched two large Jap submarines pass by, manned by American crews. The occupation was proceeding rapidly and without incident.

For the first few weeks of the occupation, the Japanese fishing fleet remained inactive within Tokyo Bay. I suspect this immobility was due largely to the fear of American occupation forces. Gradually, however, more fishermen ventured outside the Bay. Soon Japanese fishing vessels lost their worry of Americans and approached our ships for food in exchange for souvenirs.

Buried in my memory is my one and only trip ashore during the occupation. I visited a small seaside village near our anchorage. As I wandered about the dirt streets of this ancient village, I saw total ruin everywhere. The exception was a small Catholic church located on a hill in the center of town. It was obvious that the villagers were short of food. Just off one of the main streets I came upon an emaciated town beggar sitting cross-legged on a pile of trash and garbage. He was smoking a cigarette and was nothing but skin and bones. He was obviously starving. I was observing a fellow human being sifting through fly-infested garbage in a struggle to exist. As sorrow gripped my heart, I thought of an old Robert Burns quotation , "Man's inhumanity to man makes countless thousands mourn."

Wherever I wandered that day, to my surprise I witnessed no outward signs of hostility or opposition to our occupation forces. Before returning to my ship, I visited a local steam bath filled with nude men and women. It was apparent that this village's local health spa was a place for the villagers to meet and socialize, a custom quite foreign to Americans. I also had the opportunity to visit a local tea house. Like most Japanese buildings, its dimensions were diminutive. I bruised my head twice while entering and leaving.

When I returned to the *Fraser* late that afternoon, I watched a launch full of released American prisoners pass by en route to a nearby hospital ship for rehabilitation. Notwithstanding their years of bondage and their

Dangerous Seas

emaciated appearance, they were joyous over their recent release from military prison. Their nightmare was over. They were free and headed for home. As the launch neared a hospital ship, in their honor a military band began to play patriotic songs "America, the Beautiful," "Yankee Doodle," "Dixie," and "My Country 'Tis of Thee." These familiar melodies brought tears to the eyes of the repatriated Americans. It was a very emotional scene. I couldn't help but think of home and the many blessings that have been our common lot. I thought about the true meaning of freedom which is freely and automatically granted to all of our citizens. One has to see how other people live to fully appreciate our country.

Dangerous Seas

V-J Day and Post War Activities

September 2, 1945 was V-J Day. That morning I watched Allied leaders being ferried to the *Missouri* where General McArthur would conduct the surrender ceremonies. Promptly at 9:33 a.m. an eight-paragraph text was signed by all parties. After almost 45 months of inexorable horror, our conflict with the Japanese was over. The war in the Pacific was officially ended.

Shortly after Japan's surrender, Tokyo Bay was jammed with warships ranging from small fleet auxiliaries to battleships. Warships were everywhere. The harbor was alive with activity. Launches and whale boats putt-putted among anchored vessels delivering men and supplies; public address systems blared announcements and orders; shrill boatswains' pipes filled the air as ships' crews went about their duties. It was late afternoon and the *Fraser* was preparing to get underway for another mine sweeping mission. We were still at anchor when I received a call from the bridge. Signalman First Class Hal Briggs was on duty and informed me that a personal message was coming in from a ship on the other side of the Bay. Once on the bridge, I saw a blinking light on the horizon spelling out a message to me. It was garbled, but it mentioned Wesleyan, my fraternity, Psi Upsilon, and it was signed by my old college classmate, Chuck Ash. Chuck was a quartermaster on the flag ship, *USS Macon*, anchored about five miles away. He was suggesting a get-together.

Personal messages by light were now permissible, provided our ship was anchored and these messages did not interfere with official navy communications. At that very moment over the P.A. system came orders to get underway. As the *Fraser*'s anchor chains rattled in the chocks in preparation for sea duty, I could not respond to Chuck's inquiry. We were leaving Tokyo Bay for an extended mine sweeping operation in the Yellow Sea.

Some weeks later the *Fraser* returned to Tokyo Bay. I decided that a reunion with Chuck Ash might be possible. I checked the roster of ships in the Bay and found that Chuck's vessel was still anchored in the same spot. As I recall, his ship was a fleet auxiliary. She was also a flag ship with an admiral aboard. This meant she was a ship of importance.

Even though we were now at peace, the navy did not look kindly on enlisted men making social visits about the harbor. Nevertheless, I found my opportunity to leave the *Fraser* on a Sunday morning when I signed up for church call. Usually, only ships larger than a destroyer had the facilities for Sunday church services. Along with other shipmates, I boarded a launch headed directly for an empty troop transport moored nearby. Our party of enlisted men climbed the starboard gangway of the transport, at which point I quickly left our group. Unnoticed, I hurried to the ship's port side and descended its ladder into a waiting launch headed for parts unknown.

From this point forward, I begged rides from a net tender, a small tug, a barge, and several launches, and at last reached my destination, the *USS Macon*. I climbed the starboard gangway, saluted the fantail, the officer of the deck, and requested where I might find Quartermaster Chuck Ash. I was told he was on watch on the bridge. I climbed several ladders to reach the bridge, and to my surprise I found my old pal stretched out on a makeshift mattress. He was stripped to the waist and sunning himself when he dozed off. It was good to see an old friend so far from home. In the time allowed, we reminisced about college days. We also discussed our post-war plans. Chuck expressed the hope of returning to Wesleyan for his degree. This time he would stay clear of science courses, particularly physics. With a laugh, he claimed the distinction of being the only student in Wesleyan's history who took the same physics course twice, getting an "F" each time.

The hour was now late and it was time for me to return to the *Fraser*. I expressed concern about my transportation back to my ship. Chuck replied that the admiral's barge might be used. He said the admiral was ashore for the day and the coxswain of the barge was a good friend. Without further delay these arrangements were made. At the gangway I bid farewell to Chuck and boarded the waiting launch.

The admiral's barge was a luxurious craft. She was about 25 long, her hull was a spotless battleship grey and her decks shone in the sun. The forward part of the cockpit was covered by a rich navy blue canopy. The coxswain was wearing his dress blues and khaki puttees, and was standing in the stern on a raised railed platform by the helm. Aft of the coxswain was a large, blue ensign with two white stars fluttering in a spanking breeze. As I took my seat under the canopy, I noticed the boat's orderliness: boat hooks were neatly stowed, all lines correctly coiled, life preservers in place, and the boat's brass parts glowed like gold. I settled comfortably on leather-like cushions under the canopy and quickly recognized that as an enlisted man I was traveling in style.

I must point out that the navy has always had its traditions, protocol, and formalities, particularly in peacetime. In contrast, ship's etiquette to the "tin can" sailor on a destroyer was normally not adhered to. Rarely did ship's crew ever see an admiral or even an admiral's barge. But today would be different.

As our launch headed directly for the *Fraser*, anchored in a destroyer section of Tokyo Bay, I noticed that en route the admiral's ensign of two stars attracted the attention of the many ships we passed. As we approached the *Fraser*'s starboard side, all hell broke loose. Over the P.A. system came the announcement, "Admiral's barge approaching, Attention on deck!" Immediately boatswains' pipes shrilled and ships' bells sounded. Deck hands stopped their chipping and painting to stand at attention. Out of

Dangerous Seas

curiosity, those off watch appeared topside to view the approaching pageantry. Down from the bridge came the captain and the executive officer to join the officer of the deck at the gangway to greet the arriving dignitaries. All eyes strained anxiously to see what high-ranking officer of the United States Navy would emerge from under the canopy. Could it be someone famous like Admiral "Bull" Halsey or possibly Admiral of the Fleet, Chester Nimitz? Instead, up the ladder came Sonarman Third Class Williams. The captain seemed confused and retreated at once to the bridge; the executive officer was startled and muttered, "Well, I'll be damned," while the crew was overcome with uproarious laughter.

During the months of September and October, the *Fraser*, with a large mine sweeping task force and Japanese pilots, went back to Okinawa to sweep mines. After a short stay we returned to Japan where we entered Kit Suido, the entrance to the Yellow Sea. In the distance we sailed by the cities of Wakayama, Osaka, and Robe. We anchored at Sasebo Ko, Japan's large naval base in the Yellow Sea.

Even though our mine sweeping operations were no longer interrupted by enemy aircraft, unexploded mines remained a hazard to all ships. The navy asked for volunteers to sail some auxiliary vessels loaded with empty oil drums through some of the swept mine fields to test the effectiveness of our sweeping operations. The reward for this dangerous duty was an earlier honorable discharge from the navy. To me, this short term adventure had little appeal. I didn't volunteer.

On November 16th, when we returned to Sasebo Ko following one of our journeys at sea, the *Fraser*'s crew received startling good news from COMINPAC (Commander Of Mine Craft Pacific). Mine Division Seven (*Fraser*, *Shannon*, and *Bauer*) were to be reassigned to the East Coast. This directive meant we would be returning to the United States.

About the same time the point system for demobilization was announced by the navy. This system granted certain points for age, marital status, dependent children, time spent in the service, and time spent overseas. I also learned that men not having a total of 36 points currently could be transferred to other ships in MINPAC. I was in this category. The news of the navy's point system spread like wildfire. Everyone was anxious to go home and be discharged. Our ship's radio was flooded with calls inquiring about the accumulated points of various petty officers. Every ship in the harbor knew the *Fraser* was headed for the States, so we were a prime target for these calls. In short, my position on the *Fraser* was vulnerable.

Five days later, November 20th, I received orders for an immediate transfer to the destroyer *Endicott DMS 35* which was presently tied along side of the *Fraser*. I was thunderstruck by this sudden turn of events. The *Fraser* was going home; the *Endicott* was headed into the Yellow Sea on another mine sweeping mission. Reluctantly, I packed my sea bag and relocated my gear in the crews' quarters of the *Endicott*, my new home. It was Thanksgiving, and I was feeling sorry for myself. Meanwhile, the *Fraser* displayed her homeward bound pennant and I was not aboard. I was totally demoralized.

By chance, the day after Thanksgiving, Commander Atkins, the *Fraser*'s skipper, came over to the *Endicott* for a conference. Taking the bull by the horns and violating navy regulations, I approached Commander Atkins to plead my case to be transferred back to the *Fraser*. I carefully explained that I originally came aboard the *Fraser* when she was commissioned in Boston better than a year ago. I added that the *Fraser* had several crew members who had much less tenure than I. He listened to my request with patience and some sympathy. He replied that he would take the matter under advisement. He then returned to the *Fraser*, and I wondered what effect, if any, my plea had made. A day later I was surprised and overjoyed to learn that I was immediately reassigned to the *Fraser*.

In retrospect, I never had the opportunity to thank Commander Atkins for his kindness. Fifty years later, while writing this narrative, I thought about sending him a belated note of thanks, but regretfully I learned that he was no longer living. He was a fine captain, a quiet leader, and a good human being, much loved by his shipmates. I will always remember his helpful hand on my behalf.

Dangerous Seas

Homeward Bound

December 2, 1945, was a memorable day for the officers and crew of the *Thomas E. Fraser*. Promptly at 8: 00 a.m., Mine Division Seven, *Fraser*, *Shannon*, and *Bauer*, left Sasebo Ko with homeward bound pennants proudly streaming from our masts. We were at attention in dress blues, as our three departing ships rendered honors to our flag ship, destroyer *Gwin* and the cruiser *Oklahoma City*. In the background a military band was playing familiar melodies, "California, Here I Come," and "Auld Lang Syne." It was a brisk, chilly day of embarkation. We bade a final farewell to Japan.

Our journey to the east coast of The United States would take the better part of a month. However, for a change our voyage would be a trip of rest, relaxation, and some enjoyment knowing that our wartime adventures were finally over. My thoughts were of home and the future, but I also thought about where we had been. The men on the *Fraser* were lucky. We witnessed warfare, but escaped unscathed. I also remembered those navy and marine comrades who would never return to their homes, and a quotation from an anonymous author crept into my mind.

> They shall grow not old
> As we are left to grow old,
> Age shall not weary them
> Nor the years condemn
> At the going down of the sun
> And in the morning
> We shall remember them.

I closed my eyes and saw the marines storming ashore on Iwo Jima on that fateful day of February 19, 1945, while navy and marine pilots gave us protection against the kamikaze over Okinawa. My gratitude towards marines can best be summed up in the words of Major General Julian Smith who said, "I never again can see a United States Marine without experiencing a feeling of reverence."

My retrospection took me back to General MacArthur's moving words of September 1945 when he said, "A great tragedy has ended. A great victory has been won. The skies no longer rain death—the seas bear only commerce—men everywhere walk upright in the sunlight. The entire world is at peace. The holy mission has been completed. And in reporting this to you, the people, I speak for the thousands of silent lips forever stilled among the jungles and beaches and in the waters of the Pacific which marked their way."

Our course from Japan took us southeast, passing about 250 miles south of Iwo Jima. Our squadron of three ships then crossed the northern tip of the Marianas to Enewetok in the Marshall Islands, a journey of 2,367 miles.

Our next stops were Pearl Harbor, San Diego, and the Panama Canal. We then passed by the West Indies and sailed north to our final destination, Norfolk, Virginia. At 5:00 p.m. on January 8, 1946, the *Fraser* dropped her lines to Escort Piers. She reached her home port safely after a lengthy journey of 80,000 miles over a period of 16 months and 18 days.

A few weeks later, along with thousands of returning veterans, I received final orders to report to Lido Beach, Long Island to be discharged from the navy. I remember my last day aboard the *Fraser*. With my sea bag and captured Japanese rifle shouldered, I bade farewell to my shipmates, gave final salutes to the colors on the fantail and the officer of the deck. I crossed the gangway for the last time to a waiting bus. As I climbed aboard, I looked back once more at the *Thomas E. Fraser*. She was still a beautiful, sleek ship with graceful lines. In the words of John Paul Jones, she was a "fast ship" and she went "in harm's way" and served us well.

Dangerous Seas

Epilogue

When I was discharged from the United States Navy in 1946, I returned to Wesleyan University to complete my education. From there I went on to spend 45 years earning a comfortable living in the business world. Now I am retired and I look back at three-quarters of a century, a span of life which stirs nostalgia and gives me time to reflect.

I began these memoirs 50 years after World War II with only my family in mind as readers. In 1946, my father had suggested this project. Now my narrative has been completed and I regret that he isn't living to see the results of my efforts.

In retrospect, my generation has been amply filled with adventure and change. We witnessed the aftermath of World War I, the Great Depression, Prohibition, the Model T, electricity in the homes, refrigeration, radio, the Atomic Age, television, computers, stunning advances in sciences and technology, the rise and fall of Communism, and now a Space Age where satellites search the infinite universe.

During the great global conflict of the 1940s, we were idealistic, innocent youth who were taught the weapons of war in order to face the challenges and charges thrust upon us. World War II ended in September of 1945 at the cost of more than 40 million lives. It was the greatest tragedy in human history.

Those of us who were part of this moment in history are now disappearing one by one. Today, with the emergence of new generations, places like Iwo Jima and Okinawa will be remembered primarily by historians and a vanishing number of aging veterans. My brush with history occurred when I watched in awe as young marines stormed the beaches of Iwo Jima on February 19, 1945. I have relived that day many times. Four days later, to the cheers from surrounding ships, I saw the American flag raised atop Mt. Suribachi. In only 36 days this battle incurred total American casualties of 25,851 on eight-and-a-half square miles of rock and sprawl of warm sand. It was a shattering and blood-soaked military operation the likes of which mankind will probably never see again.

The final battle of the war took place on the island of Okinawa and in the sea around it. On land the American 10th Army, supported by marines and the Fifth Fleet, took 81 days to win a victory. At sea the most terrifying feature of the Okinawan campaign was the Japanese suicide plane. In 81 days the 10th Army lost 7,032 killed, 181 missing, and 31,081 wounded. The navy, including the British fleet, lost 22 major warships; 254 were damaged. The U.S. Navy had 49,087 killed and 4,824 wounded. Almost all of the naval casualties were inflicted by Japanese air power. To me, these momentous and painful events of history will remain in my mind forever. All other episodes of the war pale beside them. In my own destroyer mine layer squadron of twelve ships, only three emerged undamaged by enemy action: *Smith (DM 23), Wiley (DM 29),* and my own ship, *Fraser (DM 24).*

Although these searing memories of long ago are fading into yesterday's dreams, I can still see the mighty grey ships of an armada stretching to the horizon in all directions. I also remember a curious tingle when I watched the raising of the colors.

And in quiet moments, I sometimes hear the remote but bewitching melodies of a military band and the thunder of distant guns.

Today, my wife Fran and I keep a home on the banks of the Connecticut River, in the quiet village of Suffield. To avoid the long and harsh New England winters, we escape to Vero Beach, Florida where we enjoy outdoor living by the sea.

But my mind is still adrift with the momentous upheaval that we remember as WW II. And it will remain so as long as I am alive.